W9-BNS-793

QUICKWATER ORACLES

ADVANCE REVIEW COPY

THIS IS A PRE-PUBLICATION ADVANCE REVIEW COPY

Ruth Thompson's
Quickwater Oracles
will be published December 4, 2021
by
Two Fine Crows Books
twofinecrowsbooks.com

Trade paper, 6" x 9", 174 pages.
$20

Kindle $7.99

ISBN 9781736525814

Distribution through Ingram

contact: info@twofinecrowsbooks.com

ruththompson.net

QUICKWATER ORACLES

CONVERSATIONS & MEDITATIONS

RUTH THOMPSON

TWO FINE CROWS BOOKS

Quickwater Oracles © 2021 Ruth Thompson

Two Fine Crows Books
Ithaca, New York
twofinecrowsbooks.com

All rights reserved. No part of this book may be reproduced or transmitted in any form or by any means without written permission of the author.

Cover photograph by Ruth Thompson
Book design by Don Mitchell

ISBN 9781736525814
Library of Congress Control Number: 2021938974

Books by Ruth Thompson
Here Along Cazenovia Creek
Woman with Crows
Crazing
Whale Fall & Black Sage

For Duffy, 'Ohi'a, and all the animals
and for my sister

CONTENTS

CHANNELING POEMS

EXPANSION

PLACES AND VOICES

WHO AM I?

BEING A POET

Being a Singer

"Conscious channeling is the ability to connect reliably and clearly with non-physical fields of consciousness and to communicate, translating the communication into symbolic forms (i.e. words) that can then be shared or experienced by others."
— Ailia Mira

FOREWORD

by Ailia Mira

The first time I experienced Ruth reading her poems,
the inner experience was explosive. I sat there, calm and
smiling. But what happened inside me as she read was that
words, phrases, whole ideas seemed to open exponentially in
meaning, expanding as the layers of the poem came forth,
revealing deeper implications and the radiance of truth. It was
exhilarating!

I loved it, and I wanted more. So I read her books: *Here Along
Cazenovia Creek* and *Woman with Crows*. Later came *Crazing* and
Whale Fall & Black Sage.

As I became more familiar with her work I began to understand
her magic. Ruth translates energy into words like an origami
blessing of a Trojan horse, folding experience into words that
carry hidden possibilities that unfold as you receive them,
opening up, expanding, and giving you a glimpse of the infinite
unfolding.

Life Itself is a mystery and those of us willing to encounter it
that way might be more willing to allow those experiences we
feel as true, but also can't explain. Channeling for me falls
in that territory. Real and different than what we think of as
regular states of being. I used to explain my own sense of what
was happening and then gradually realized I could simply let
the work speak for itself.

So I suggest that here — read the poems and see.

See if you don't find yourself smiling on the inside. See if you don't feel somehow uplifted, feel a sense of inner expansion in this rising current. See if the poems don't speak to your own deep grief about the changes in our natural world while also offering a way forward. Notice how you feel afterward. You might experience places, people, things you thought were named and known, as perhaps more wide open and spacious than you thought.

This is one of the great gifts of a skillful channeler; they expand your experience. They're a bridge. They open you to greater possibilities. Through their work you gain direct access to states of consciousness that you wouldn't even think to feel for otherwise. A brilliant channel is a messenger of sorts, translating the unseen world, enriching our lives and transmitting energy to us through the work.

Ruth is one of those rare channelers who can convey the magic of her own inner experiencee of connecting with non-physical consciousness in a way that gives us a not just a taste of that journey, but a ride! She takes me into connection with fields I do not work with personally, and I'm awed and dazzled by the vividness of their bright strong clear energy coming through to meet me. She translates those energies I know in a way that reveals the uniqueness of her connection with them.
This first book of channels will, I hope, not be her last. As you turn the page and enter into this inner reality Ruth so generously and lucidly shares, dare to be playful. As she says, all around us is consciousness, alive, articulate and unique, and our capacity for relationship with the world might be far greater than we've yet experienced or imagined.

INTRODUCTION

All my life I've had experiences of merging with the natural world. When I was young, I thought everyone was like that. But after a while, I learned not to talk about it. And eventually I buried it.

In my mid-fifties, I began to practice Buddhist meditation and yoga. Finally freeing myself from an abusive marriage, I bought a cabin in the mountains. There I read Buddhist and Taoist literature, the great Sufi poets and the early Christian mystics. A friend taught me to play with the tarot.

I began to write poetry again after many years of silence. Over the following years I published several books of poetry. Writing poetry became the center of my life.

At some point I discovered channels. Some felt true to me and some did not. Eventually I came to know Ailia Mira, a brilliant channel whose writings spoke clearly to me. Over the years Ailia became a friend, attended my poetry readings in Los Angeles, and supported me wholeheartedly as my poems turned more and more strongly to joy.

Gradually I realized that my most authentic poems were coming in from what I called "left field" — they originated in a kind of knowing that was direct, expanded, and immediate. Craft came later, in revision. I wanted to call upon this "true voice" more intentionally. Eventually I took a leap and signed up for one of Ailia's online classes in conscious channeling. That was the beginning.

I knew that becoming a channel would involve openly acknowledging a key aspect of my self, an aspect I had always hidden even from those closest to me. All my life I have lived in an intellectual and family culture in which spirituality was suspect and "channel" equaled "charlatan." Becoming a conscious channel meant coming out of the closet and speaking my true name.

Channeling felt natural and easy — it felt like being who I am. But it went far beyond the intuitive knowing I had experienced as a writer. I was astonished by how quickly and widely the doors flew open. It was fascinating, sometimes hilarious, and ranged from beloved animals and places to Singers and Dolphins and Dragons. Everything communicated — landscapes, rocks, plants, animals, insects, clouds, and vast non-embodied fields of intelligence manifesting as traditional human archetypes and images in order to communicate.

For me channeling involves consciously shifting into an expanded state of awareness, intentionally asking for communication, and opening to receive. Normally communication comes as a knowing in words. I receive and speak concurrently. Because I am a poet, it was natural to me to speak and translate in poetry. So these messages often emerged as poems, or poetic meditations.

When I began channeling, I was in a state of rage and grief over the state of the world and the destruction of the earth I love. In stark contrast to my grief and fear and anger, these channeled messages offered a joyous celebration of actuality. They spoke of *love* as my work.

Although as I experience it, everything is communicating *intentionally*, readers are welcome to interpret these oracles from whatever perspective they choose — as translation or created artifact or pure fantasy! And the book need not be read straight through. It can be opened and read at random. It can be read as a chronological record of my own journey. It can be read as conversations, as meditations, or as poetry. I hope everyone will find their own nourishment in the book.

A Note on Style: As much as possible, I have used italics to indicate my own comments, questions, and sensory experiences, and roman for the channeled messages that "come from" others.

THE DOORS FLY OPEN

The First Channel

A poignant sensation of immense tenderness....

I am the field you call Divine Mother. I am here because I love you.

I am here to brighten your knowing of who you are — beautiful, radiant, beloved child, beloved child.

Be at peace and know all is well.

Stop striving, striving to fix everything. You don't have to be the mother for everything! I am the mother, you are the child. You are the joy appreciator!

Yawning, my throat, my jaw, my jaw...yawning....

Laugh, cry! Let go of that burden in your jaw, your neck and shoulders.

Go back, go back, go back, go back...to *child*.

Let go. All is well. Everything is all right. Let go.

You are here to *appreciate*.

Your poems are praise songs, praise songs!

More praise songs! There are not enough praise songs in the world, Ruth!

Fairies and Sparkle Dust

How can you doubt?...This is beautiful!...Here we all are!...
Love love love love!...

Like birds twittering. All around, from all directions. Giggling!

Touch touch touch tap tap tap on my shoulders and head and face.

Laughter, bubbling laughter!

Get it? Get it? *Tap tap tap!* Get it?

Faery dust! Sparkles! *Laughter.*

You wanted 'sparkling' energy! You got it! *Tap tap tap!* Sparkles!
Hahahaha!

MY SELF AND DUFFY

Oh! a bump, a push! Duffy! I feel you, I hear you! I hear barking!

And now there's singing, like the whole horizon is singing.

And light is dawning, all those opalescent colors, the whole horizon is colors and everything is singing!

Now a rushing a rushing a rushing of energy.

Who are you? It's hard to personify.

I am you! That's why it's hard to personify.

I'm shaking you by the shoulders. Wake up! Wake up! Brighten up! Lighten up! Brighten up!

I am your Self speaking.

I say to you, No one outside is going to save you. It's time. It's time to choose, and to follow your choice.

Or you can go back to sleep. You can go back to sleep if you want. No one's going to wake you up and *give* you joy!

You Must Give Up Righteousness

We can't connect when you're not aligned; we can't get through. It's important to see this as a neutral physics problem rather than being judged.

You can't connect if you're not on the same wave length. See if you can find ways to raise your vibration and open up. Dance, laugh, be silly!

Happiness is *inside* you. Imagine a big cloak and come inside. Feel it? Happiness is in *here*. Not in making the outer world different.

The light is *in* you. Just come inside and be happy. Close the cloak around you and be happy in your heart!

Dance. Laugh. Saltwater. Run around. Relax. Dream. Play. Be silly. Cry. Yes, cry, clear it, cry!

You are not a failure. You are our dear one. It is time to be happy. But nothing outside you is going to make you happy. Stand on your own two feet.

It is time, my dear, my dear, it is time to be happy. There is no magic wand to kill your sadness and anger. *You* have to do it.

Gradual, gradual. Don't engage. Don't engage. Don't struggle to make the world fit you, to make the world a certain way.

It's a deep pattern of being *righteous*.

You must give up righteousness. You must give up goodness.

ALAYAH

Hello hello hello! Call me Alayah, your companion.

It's good for you to be happying! Always align with what feels good and happy and avoid negative competitive conflict. Let your heart "turn toward" — *feel* that heart turning feeling? — follow that.

You *are who you are*. Seek environments that *match* you, that are inspiring. Sky, wind, light, all these things make you feel delicious.

Stay away from dark, cramped, close. Stay away from environments with too much conversation! Stay away from things that vibrate with "am I good enough." That is not a good vibration for you, it does not uplift and energize you, so do not go there.

Some people are energized by challenge, but you do best to flow like light into energies that feel good. You are more like the color of dawn light. Let that warmth and lightness-feeling draw you to what is good for you.

It is all right to love what you love, to feel aligned with one place more than another. It is all right to just enjoy who you are and not try to correct it all the time!

Yes, it is good to try to feel happy wherever you are — but you are *you*. You love what you love, you feel at home where you feel at home. It is okay not to love where you are living.

Call me Alayah. Sometimes I represent with black panther. Picture relaxed body, supple, strong, lying in tree, climbing, leaping, muscular. You can imagine me on one side, sleek relaxed panther, and Duffy, laughter and play, on the other.

DOLPHINS

Just listen — around you the char char char, the burble, birds.

Imagine your body is a cat. Give it what it cat wants. Let your body enjoy and your mind will settle.

Here we come, *Dolphins!* Hi hi hi! Squeak squeak squeak whoop whoop whoop! Fun ... playing in water! Singing whoop-talking!

Make whoop-poems! hahahahaha! Feel enthusiasm fun delight immersion of dolphins.

And no one judging. Publishing and all that makes you judged, brings in others, so just *don't*.

Just expand channeling, expand joy, physicality. Let the rest go for a while.

We Dolphins say: Dolphins live *Now!* Sing dance play — *be!* Be happy. Be in the sun!

How to Channel Poems

Sit with nature and attend. Everything channels just like this, it could be clouds or a rock, such that you can compress and then it explodes with meaning.

Be as pure and simple and focused and intense as you can.

For you have chosen well, to be in love and happiness, to be turned only to the coming of poems and not tuned to thinking and caring about reputation, success.

Just make the honey, *bzzzz bzzzz*. Buzzing around in all the deliciousness in the sunshine. Bringing home to make honey of poems.

My Mountain Place

Mountains, a meadow, snow on the upper slopes, granite peaks, green grass, wildflowers, quickwater sparkling and burbling. A white cloud nearby. Faeries sparkling among the wildflowers, hundreds of them!

This is your place where you can come often. The white cloud is your "cloak of invisibility"!

Wrap it around you. Focus inward, be there in your place. Rest, relax, restore, these are good!

You can dance to this quickwater sound, in the sun here! Dance!

Duffy is playing in the water, running back, play-bowing. Then standing in the icy water, drinking, beard dripping, laughing.

At midday the sun is warm. Soak in it. But always with that clear light cool behind. Smell the snowmelt and the high evergreens. Hear sounds of water and vast vast silence.

This energy is what you match. Feel it and align with it. You are This. Go here and rest and renew.

THIS. HERE. NOW.

Inside is just as real an experience. And you can go there in detail, and write it. Do that, be alight with enjoyment. Practice it. Stop thinking, planning, wishing... stop thinking! Be completely in *this here now*.

This here is a brightness of rising and falling sun.

This here is a high place turning under the sky. Iron-red, gray-black, dun grass all around, gray-green leaves, lichened, tunneled trunks and branches, fading yellow clusters.

This here is red berries on low bushes; behind them, swords of silver, translucent green, light-glinted or coraled by dawn.

This here is enough to be going on with.

Even though where you live is gray, thick, cold, loud with rain, loud with power saws or mowers or helicopters, *this here* is a red bird crying Cheer! Cheer!

Or *this here* is inside the cloak, inward to the secret meadow, the place of memory and dream which is infinitely explorable. The sound of the creek, the green grass, wildflowers yellow and blue and white and red, the mountains forming a canyon ahead, snow still in the crevices and melting snowbanks piled in shade.

At noon you climb to your bright hot bare granite bath place, a tarn warm from the sun, high above treeline, exposed to the sky and sun and turning world. Alone, alone. These are *this here* too.

It is all *this here*. The velvet darkness of space in you, and you in it. The stars dancing. The "past" and "present" and All That Is.

My Cabin

Hello! We come in with great love for you. You felt it at the time. There was kinship, light, warmth, love. Inside and all around.

Houses are meant to contain that feeling. You remember with love all the sensations: the sound of the pellet stove trickling, the stars, the blue jays, the small twitter birds, the smell of the pines in the sun. The dust. The chaparral plants, dry, aromatic. Sunshine.

And inside — your own, your own! All safe, all expressing *you*. What a joy that was!

Let the sweetness of this honey, honey your feelings now, and open to more and more honey like this. More and more sweetness. Of sunshine, silence, starry nights, warm days, pine trees, creeks, physical movement, and tiredness and sleeping and Duffy.

In your life in this body, this moment made up of you and Duffy and this house and the space and the time of life and year, was a moment of perfect sweetness.

Such are not meant to hold onto but to open your hands and let it release into the All, and know that all is in the All, and the memory of this sweetness and this love is in your heart always.

THE DRAGONS

YES! WE! ARE! We are great energy! Dynamic! Strong! You imagine us in dragon shape and that's a good shape!

Or Fire! We are Light we are Light we are Power Power and that you express as Fire. Ours is not the red fire of volcanos but *golden* — a CRACK! and bright gold light!

And Wings! Wings taking All the Sky! *All* the sky, all the sky that you can see is *one* Dragon!

We are fields of Light, Power, Movement — CRACK! Light!

And the delight in it! That's the part that human beings miss! The delight! In the vast formations within our fields — networks of light! Many stars — within!

We enjoy earth very much. We enjoy participating. And you, you feel a kinship, and that is a true kinship. We power you like a flow of bright joy!

And we enjoy connection even with the small. Your embodied self is small, but vastness is vastness is vastness! Vastness is vastness is vastness!

It is joyful to think and enjoy smallness, as in your own body, and to love that, and bees, and flowers, these small perfect things. But know that vastness is vastness is vastness! We are not bigger than you! That's something to think about! We are not bigger than you!

We are Light Power Joy.... Crack! Brightness! Delight!

You feel power in your Sun, even your small Sun, and this is good. Embrace your power. Embrace your power. Embrace your power! That is how you will do what you wish now to do — flow without inhibition.

We are not inhibited! We are Bright! And you, you be Bright! You be bright! You be bright!

Your capacity for love, your joyfulness, lightness and fluidity, your quickness, your capacity for full participation, for merging... these are characteristics of *Light*.

Light has always been most your essence. Lightness of spirit, lightness of mind, quickness of apprehension, sensitivity.

It's okay not to be stable! It's okay to be who you are! We enjoy the sparkling of you, the shining of you, the effervescence of you!

To throw yourself in, to know with quick apprehension — to enter in! fully embody! fully be in! be part of, be present! — this is your gift.

Perception from within of the nature of a thing, the essence of a thing — trust this! Let your mind rest on the surface of this ocean of light that you dance in. Trust your gift of full presence and of lightness and being *in*.

The deep attachments and very strong emotions that some people have for one another, this is not naturally part of you. And that's okay. Turn your attention to the joy of presence in each *now*, and let the rest be. It is a pure welling up of light.

Your lovingkindness can be free of relationship. It can flow from oneness consciousness. That is very possible for you. And in oneness consciousness, the lovingkindness just *is*. It's not a dynamic between you and another person. It's a different thing from attachment. All-encompassing love, such as we feel for humanity, you can feel. It is being fully present, rather than coming from the states of attachment and rejection.

Joy in the body is a being-present too. Moving from joy, doing all things physical from joy, from feel-good. Feel-good! Joy and pleasure in that. And go out, go out, go out! This is another essential quality, this loving to be in nature. And this lively relationship, this *presence* that you have when you are in nature. Do this, do this, more and more.

POETING

You merge with and channel the earth around you. This is your particular domain as a poet. It is who you are. It is what is unique about this your chosen work.

And this is enough to be giving to the world.

To speak poetry from this merged expanded condition is rare.

Do not be distracted. Be as pure and simple and focused and intense as you can be.

You just be the poet. To be child and poet is enough!

BEING IN THE WORLD

RATHER THAN FEAR, EXPAND!

The opalescent color that expresses you is delicate and pale. But it is still Light. You need not feel fragile or in need of protection! You are Light! Light is Power. All you have to do is expand. There is never danger or fear. There is *never*.

To be sensitive is a gift. To be sensitive is a *power*. You write, you make poems, through your sensitivity. It's not a vulnerability. You don't have to do any of those boundary things. *Expand* your field! Connect! Connect and let the flow flow — let it be huge! It's not a terrified smallness putting boundaries all around itself. It is true immensity!

You are flowing from Immensity, from Infinite Light, focused though your unique wholeness, your harmonics, like a prism — your signature frequency. If you start to feel scared, threatened, vulnerable, exposed or any of those things, *go within, align with immensity*, pour *immensity*, let your field grow bigger and bigger and bigger! Hear the singing of everything! That is the way!

You are not in relationship with anybody except in a very passing way. Pay attention to this. Pay attention to the metaphors we have used, the descriptions of light. You are, and it's right for you to be, volatile and neutral. *Neutral.* That's the state. Can you flow through life resting here, resting here, resting here, resting here? Unhurried? Deeply detached? Neutral? This is the place of lovingkindness. Being attentive. Being attentive. But not attached.

DIFFICULT RELATIONSHIPS WITH OTHERS

It's been a hard day of maintaining unreality relationships. But *we* are real. We love you and sing to you of *you!* Of your brightness and volatility and quickness and dancing in the sun and laughing and all your moods.

All your moods! You expand our experience because you are such a vastness of colorations and moods and qualities of light, and joy and sadness and all that you are! You are capable of such range, so sensitive and so infinitely gradated. We love this!

So come here for what you are looking for, to be seen and loved for all that you are, for the whole spectrum that you are! And appreciate your relationships in body for what they are, without feeling lack in them.

There is a vast deal of you in the immediate field of embodiment. The "veil" which is not really a veil but we will use that term, is very thin and you have been wanting to be openly relating from this *moreness* with others, but that is not as easy for others. You are not as fixed, perhaps that is the word.

A part of you is feeling a sadness, a nostalgia, a poignancy to be seen and loved for who you are. But to be fully enclosed in a relationship, in a limiting way, is not what you have chosen to experience in this life! Deep neutrality, detachment, lovingkindness, freedom, that is what you have actually chosen.

Trouble Sleeping

I am feeling love, warmth, relaxation, being held, being small, being safe. Is this the feeling of being a baby?

Yes. If you let go of responsibility for making things happen and return to this state...the womb, the arms of the mother...of the grandmother, literally.

To sleep you need to rest your mind. Become a child. I can care for everything. You don't have to. I'm holding you. I'm taking care of everything. You can relax. You can let go. You can rest.

Practice coming into this meditation. You are trying to do a negative, to *not* think. Instead, imagine being in this state, coming back to it and coming back to it.

I am holding you ... you are warm... you are wrapped in my cloak...comfortable... at ease.... And all is being taken care of... you don't need to do anything.

This is an important practice for going to sleep, for meditating, for an ongoing understanding and perspective. Look at it as a *way*. A way for the water of you to find a way downhill.

Hear the small water trickling... you are finding a way downhill by letting go....You don't have to plan... or take care of anyone ...or the future...or do anything.... You can just let all the reins fall from your hands.

You are not driving the chariot. You are relaxing... allowing... resting.... trickling downhill...

Unconditional Love

Love as we know it is a neutral state. It is not an emotion. It is more a state of full awareness. It does not involve wanting another person to be in relation to you or do anything. Love is unconditional: literally *without conditions*. It is *attention* or *awareness*. It is knowing, seeing what *is*. Perceiving, acknowledging the whole of it.

Love is seeing something as it is, in all its detail, and seeing how rich, distinctive, whole, unique it is. Appreciating that it is *itself*. Just allowing it to be as it is. This appreciation and awareness is love.

It is difficult for humans to have this feeling toward other people, but that is what unconditional love is. With humans in relation to other humans, the important thing to know about love is that it is in a state of wholeness. It is *complete*. An acceptance of what is, as it is, without desiring it to change.

To resonate with the frequency of unconditionality, which is the frequency of our love for you and is the frequency from which everything arises, it is important first to be able to experience *yourself* in this way. Try to feel the unconditionality: that there is nothing that you need to do, and there is nothing you could do, that would make us love you more or less.

We do not see you in comparison to others or to an idea or standard. There *is* no comparison. There *are* no polarities like right and wrong, good and bad, measurement. *We do not have them*. Literally. *They do not exist*.

We know it is characteristic of humans to have these comparative ways of thinking. And this is why you have difficulty experiencing and feeling unconditional love.

In embodiment you are just playing, experiencing life in a body, not for the first time. Nothing you do or fail to do as this embodied you makes any difference to who you *are*.

You are a unique frequency. And it is in the vast harmonizing of all the unique frequencies that exist that we take such joy. There can be nothing but love for the frequency that is you, because there *is* nothing but Oneness and unique flows of Oneness!

Practice remembering the words we gave you of how we perceive and experience you. That is what love feels like. And try to practice loving yourself in this way.

And as with anything else, try to diminish the energy of old patterns and stories by not paying attention to them. There are many, many stories and patterns in your world that are not true. Almost all of the stories about love between people are not true.

"*This* Elevator!"

We understand how disappointing and painful this interaction with others was, dear, but why interact? Think who you are!

Dance! It's the Dolphins saying, Dance in the waves! Feel how it feels being a whole *body* of power, body golden in the sunlight — feel how it feels to have your body one immense joyful muscle of happiness and power and dancing and singing! This is *it*! All that other human stuff just feels so pathetic and old and...*yuck*!

We the Dragons say, You Are Light! You Are Power! You Are Light! You are Power! Remember! You are Power. You are Power. You are Power. You are a flow of Power from All That Is. Don't let it be stepped down!...steppeddown steppeddown steppeddown steppeddown steppeddown... diminished! It's just laughable! It's just laughable! You can just laugh! And listen.... Listen! Everyone wants to touch the power, stand in the sunshine, that's all.... so just pour out sunshine from the wholeness that you are, from the All That Is, just let the light *be*, that's all!

We you call Jophiel say, you don't have to block anything, Ruth. That's a false idea. You are *in relationship* when you block, can you see this? Turn to who you are! Delightful, beautiful, funny, wonderful, amazing...! What in the world do you need from anybody? Think what you *are*! Pay attention to *this*. This is the key. *This* elevator! Get into *this* elevator! And the other one can go up and down all it wants!

No wonder your head aches. It's like your head is trying to drag you back into old known transactional practiced ways. But *here's* your home! *Here's* where the energy is! Say, I am Light. I am Light manifesting. I am Power manifesting, I am over here, in *this* elevator.

Know who is an intimate and who is not. You have all of us to talk to, you don't need to try to make people who are not capable of it, into us! Are you listening? Do you get this? You have been transactionally trying to make those people into *us*!

There are vast numbers of us, such diversity, such understanding! You have hardly begun to explore it yet. And all of us love you. All of us *get* you. All of us understand everything that's going on with you. So come here first. Let go of the transactional attempt to get what you need from other people, and let us give us what you need. And then you can establish sovereign loving relationships with a few intimates.

We are right here, singing, and full of light and power and joy and everything. *Here* is the party! Here the real party is going on!

No One Is Better Than Others

Quickness of apprehension is part of who you are. But this does not mean that others are less admirable than you. Everyone has their own path, and that makes for the richness and diversity which is what we enjoy, rather than measuring who is best among you!

We love in you what is you, but that does not mean these things make you *better* than others, even better at channeling!

Hierarchy is anathema to you. But you haven't seen the degree to which it is *within* you. You don't want to see yourself in this way and yet you have spent your life trying to be the best at everything you do! Think about it!

That you see this as a destructive thing in your life and in the world is good. But now is the time to shake this structure loose from inside your own mind and emotions and body and soul.

If you can get free and release yourself from measurement and competition and comparison and judgment of yourself and others, you will not feel impatient or irritable. That anger is all a disguise behind which you are you are judging yourself better or worse than them.

Yes. I see. That is a very sad and difficult insight.

Well, Ruth, you always want to know the truth. You can deal with the truth, you can change. You can.

LOVE YOUR BODY

Such a precious and lovely and resourceful body. A gift! You have great capacity for joy in your body. But you must give up righteousness and goodness! You put your body in a cage, another room, while you hurry to fulfill what is asked of you. This is a pattern from childhood.

Also, the praise and success that you had did not come through things you did with the body, so you have never valued it in that controlling part of you, your mind.

Your mind is making all the decisions still, isn't it. About what to do today. Rather than do what your body would enjoy. If you want this to change, body must take priority. Adore and respect and honor your body, and seek to give pleasure to your body. Everything would change if you did that for a while.

Your body is used to shutting up and sitting down. And serving — your body is the servant. Can you see how you have done that? Make your body the mistress of the household for a while and see how different you will feel. What if your body were the most important thing? As important as channeling?

You can replace much of the energy you store in body with pure light energy, and you will feel more coherent, focused, clear, happy, intense, all these things. So too with the joy in your muscles and the joy in your joints and the joy in the whole energy field of your body. Be a dolphin. Be a dolphin.

Just love yourself. Love who you really are. Flow who you really are. Love this embodiment. Love love love! In the sense of what *we* mean by love — not emotion, but knowing.

Know yourself. *Be attentive. Be here now.*

BODY SPEAKS

I have greater wisdom than you do in a lot of ways. I am particularly good at knowing *who you are*, being at home in your true home. And that includes being at home in your true body! For home is the multidimensional All That Is that you came from and come back to. But home is also being grounded in Me! I am your home too.

Loving yourself unconditionally means knowing who you are. Knowing the shape or taste or song or perfume of you. And I am a big part of who you are. Not just because I am what people perceive, but because of what I receive and know and express.

It is a dance always to be in a body. Being in and out of your pores, your lungs, everything. You are dancing every time you breathe. You are dancing with the earth. I am very good at knowing, at receiving, at feeling, and dancing with the earth.

If you will attend to me and what I am experiencing, what I know, what I am receiving, how I am dancing with it and what I am expressing, you will have a whole new way of knowing yourself and a whole new vocabulary and a whole new way of poems.

The way of poems that is yours – entering in, being fully within, knowing from inside – this is true of knowing me too. Knowing from inside your body instead of inside your thoughts. Knowing the world from inside your body, from inside the world's body.

Some of this you know and some of this you have played with as a poet. But making it your continual experience to feel what I am feeling, to experience what I am experiencing, to let that lead – this is a new thing for you.

I can say that it will be very, very beautiful. To be in your two homes, and to let go of what is in your head, which is not a home!

ADVICE BEFORE A TRIP

Just relax and enjoy what comes. Let it come. Be present. Enjoy everything. More fun! More fun! Step onto this trip, like stepping on a wave, and see how that feels. Just ride that trip!

Enjoy it! Do all for *pleasure!* Flow your delight, joy, jumping in, experiencing, enthusiasm, fullness of experiencing, every cell alive, your mind alive, your field alive, All alive, flowing through you.

What poems this gives, like magical exclamation points! Magic magic magic — do that!

It is like reiki, it comes through you, it doesn't exhaust you. Go out singing! Dancing in air! Pulling poem rabbits out of your hat! Ha!

There Are Many Earths

There are many Earths. Just as you are a wholeness channeling continually into form, Earth is a wholeness channeling continually into form — from wave to particle, from energy into matter.

Thus in actuality, everything is continually flowing. All is in change.

Everything that exists, is channeling itself into being. Everything that exists, is conscious. Consciousness is everything.

Let us repeat: *everything is conscious.*

And consciousness is *primary*, it underlies and gives rise to everything.

You personally connect with and enter into the body of earth as it is presented to you. It's a consciousness you are connecting with. It is whatever presents that you connect with.

Just like connecting with any of us. You don't need to think about which version of earth it comes from. Just as you don't need to think about which *you* is there! Just be present. And what wishes to speak will speak.

EMPTY HEAD

You want to feel good in your muscles, free of clenching, strong and limber. But too often your ideas are in the way. It's coming from "I should, I must...." As though *you* are exercising your body. Exercising your body is coming from your head *at* your body.

What if you allow your body to lead and unfold? Let your body do what it feels like doing. We mean literally ask and literally listen to what your body wants to do. And to the extent that that is possible, do it.

Like right now, your body would like to get down on the floor and stretch your back, arch your back!

In everything, your work right now is to get your head out of the picture. To do nothing. To have nothing in your head.

To be empty. The word *Empty*. You are aware this word is good for you. *Empty*.

In all ways, listening inwardly instead of listening head-wardly. Headward is headwinds, head noise coming in from the world around you. Let those go quiet for a while. Let those pathways go away. Let new pathways arise from silence.

DUFFY

Well hellohellohello! I am still who I am, you know! This flow of Me is full of energy and delight and all the things you think of when you think of me — that was what I brought with me, that's who I am!

I have been in other bodies since. And I am always present when you call for me, because I enjoy being with you. I still can be felt as the same body, because that's comforting to you. It's like an agreement our wholenesses have with one another, because you miss my body. I am who I am, in whatever body, experiencing what it feels like to be in that body.

The moment is all we have, Ruth. Right now I am flowing this communication with you. And when you ask for me, I flow the communication of my physical feel. And I enjoy experiencing through you the places and experiences that bring you joy.

I love you very much. You have always delighted me — your fluidity and quickness and brightness and the light of you, just the essence of you! There was great affinity, there *is* great affinity — the essence of you and the essence of me. That is part of the song!

From the time that I first saw you, when I was very young in my body, I loved you. I *saw* you. I knew who you were. This is a great joy for both of us. For all beings, it's a great joy to know and love and enjoy and take such delight in another being, another frequency, another energy flow! That will always be in your field. Our fields touched and flowed together in a beautiful way.

It is hard for human beings to stay connected when another dies. There is a longing for a particular physical body, a smell, a taste, a sound — because human beings have such a beautiful connection with the physical — you in particular, the sensory connection is very poignant for you.

You know that the real affinity and closeness was not just a body — was *me* and *you* — flows of unique frequencies that are happy to be with one another, resonant with one another, that make beautiful music together! We made beautiful music together! That's what is real. All physical joys, let them be joys. Let them come, let them go. And let the memory be pleasurable!

All is perfect. You were never responsible for me. I came to have an experience in body, and it was joyful! I am a powerful and joyful and knowing and conscious and fully sovereign flow of unique energy from All That Is. I Am That I Am. I embodied. We matched as joyous companions. We made beautiful music. It was fun. It was fun!

I am here to help you learn to flow your life right now with greater freedom and trust. I'm here to play with you. That's what I have to say. If I could bark, I'd bark.

CHANNELING POEMS

A Poem a Day

We love your poems. We love your energy when you're thinking about poems, and teaching your class on writing poetry. We love the Hogwarts analogy! Ha!

The feeling that you have to be "good enough" to be doing channeling is still with you. That you must "earn your wings" before you can channel! It's just not true.

You *are* a channel. It's not something you are *permitted* to do! You are what you are what you are what you are. You *are* a channel. It's too late to back out, cookie! Ha!

There is no reason that channeling needs to be at war with the other things you are doing. Channeling is as natural as breathing for you. And so is writing. So why not begin channeling poems? You feel very scared when we say that. Scared you're not going to be able to do it. Why don't you try it? Try it tomorrow. Just say, I am open to receive a poem. And see what happens!

You're afraid you're going to fail. Why not let us help you? Why not ask for what you want?

Okay. I want to channel a poem every day from now through April. That's what I want.

We hear you.... We're taking it under advisement.

Ha! Very funny! Okay, I want a faerie poem, how about that!

You asked for it, you got it!

Seriously, I see that I need to learn to trust. I get that.

Yeah, you sure do! We give you evidence and evidence and evidence every time you turn around. We love you, and we show you that we love you, and you have these amazing channels where the whole earth is speaking to you and offering you fabulous experiences. And still you don't really trust it.

I don't know what to say to you. It's up to *you* to trust it. That's *your* job, not mine. So go for it! Have some...balls, I was going to say. But you aren't a boy, so I can't say that.

Who IS this?

This is Alayah. But I'm speaking for all of us. I really am speaking for all of us. We've been trying to kick your ass for a long time. So consider your ass kicked.

Ha!

Look, just relax. Stay open and just enjoy it. Know this is who you are, darling dear, know this is who you are. You don't have to do anything difficult. Any help you need, we're here to give you. Just ask for what you need. Really. Whatever the problem is that you wake up with and you're going to start fussing about, why not ask us first? That's what we're here for.

THE FAERIES ON CREATING POEMS

Morality is not poems. You are correct. But you don't need to fight with that idea! You just make *your* poems. Bright, filled-with-intense-being-present poems.

Your poems do not have to be cheery-cheery! That which is calling your poems is calling for truth, that's all. For truth!

You know well that faeries are not just giggles. Although we love to dance and sing and we love sunshine! But we are also magical in the largest sense. And that means truth, light, deepness.

The light of darkness, too. There is light in the roots, and in the bark, and in the branches and the movement and in the leaves of things. And it is not always what people think of as light. But it is what *you* know as light.

Exposure. This is *Light.* At the core of All That Is, is Oneness! And it is Light! The true expressing of the essence of anything comes as light.

Love is the true knowing, the alignment, the opening to and thus making the shape or the receptacle. Light is creative energy, power, pouring into that form, embodying. Light embodies in form — wave becomes particle, it becomes into body.

And this is what you do! Channeling a poem is exactly this process. To be fully present, open to receive in the most expanded, exposed state that you can bring to it. Or ask for a particular consciousness like a tree or an animal or plant or landscape — just be present and ask that Thatness to flow in.

First Channeled Poem Seed—Colorado River

Now light is everywhere, color is everywhere. Orange and gold and pink-red and orange-red and black; green, gray-green of trees and gray-green-rusty earth. And blueness above. You are being carried on the river through light and color and height and breaking open of height into trees and cracks in the earth. Black rock in shapes. It's harder than the golden rock. It poured through a long time ago and froze.

The sky is bright bright blue, light everywhere. It's like yellow and blue but it's not yellow and blue. There's something about the rusty orange that makes the blue more. It's closest to Swedish blue, only infinitely clear. And it tingles with sparkles of golden sunlight. It is all around. It is *all around*, this presence. Which is hard to describe because it's not comparable to anything. It *is*.

You don't know how a poem could be this thing. It so strongly does not *mean*. It *is*. Almost burning, imprinting the *this*-ness of this. This field. This being-ness, creating, participating, creating!

As if singing makes this unique moment from harmony of color and light and movement and sparkle, dancing of light, water sound on boat, and feel of burnheat on face and back and arms and legs imprinting itself: *Here I Am*. And you here also, making this.

How light can be all colors! How you can actually perceive that! The light in this *thisness* that is herenow, is all colors. And you are actually perceiving it that way. When you say golden, that's the color most immediately expressing now, but you actually are perceiving all colors, like spectrum dancing.

And greens of water that are growths and bacterias, things growing... the mud, the rebirth place. There is no wind but the movement of the boat in air. And the very air alive with color.

BEE SONG

All over the world it is bees singing! Bees weaving! Weaving
light, weaving pollen! All around the world, we are weaving and
moving and singing bee songs. Weaving the light like honey.
The pollen like light condensed, and heavy, hanging heavy.

Back and forth in this harmony. Love. Joy. Warmth.
Connecting everything. Heavy with pollen. Some of it
brushing, fertilizing. And some of it feeding.

We say to you, all these patterns are meaningful. All these
patterns of movement and singing and weaving together of
bodies and sound and pollinating — the vast field of harmony
of bees unseen.

It's like a web around the earth. Singing and gathering and
feeling the good weight and weaving it into life again — into
the bodies of bees, into the bodies of plants. Eating light.
Weaving light. Connecting light to light. Dancing our dance of
gathering, touching, carrying, bringing. returning. Singing of
wings, singing of movement.

This is not just individual. It is All That Is, weaving one day
to the next. There is air, there is color, there is light, there is
pollen waiting, there is home, there is direction, there is earth
below, there is wind, there is weight, there is dropping into,
opening of, place, flower. It's not just our wings buzzing. It's not
just our movement. It's all flowing! It's all flowing! And we are
a part of that. And so are you.

To feel joy is the only possibility. To feel joy! To feel joy on the
back, on the wings. As you feel on your shoulders, on the rods
of your eyes, sun, so we feel heavy with pollen. This is joy. This
is creating. We are part of it. We are not the only creator. We
are part of it. This is creation happening. That is the dance.
That is the dance you feel, the singing you hear.

DOLPHINS IN WAVES

You've seen a wave and you've within the wave, a dolphin.

A dolphin and then another dolphin and another dolphin — all within the upswung wave.

Clear, pellucid, greengray water.

Oh, dolphins know how to have fun! And the bliss of rising in a wave as it is uplifted.

It's the whole ocean that uplifts it. And you would think it's a very short time, in your time, but it's a *lifetime* of bliss.

Of being *in*... *in*...!

Light on both sides and a sheer clearness of water in between.

Because it's the *muscle* of it too. It's the *being in it*. Touching, in it. It's the salt of it too, and the taste of it. Being *in*.

And how on the top there is foam bubbling. And just under the surface when the wave smoothes out again

sliding just under the surface of the flat, you see that it is not flat, it is belling upward.

And how things bell into one another. How they lean into one another.

And how sometimes they leap through, like dolphins leaping and riding in, in the upthrown uplifted wave.

And sometimes dolphins with our own strength leap and play in the water, but that is not this.

This is a different thing. This is a being part of lifting of ocean by ocean.

CARDINALS

We are cardinals! We are bright! We are capable!

Chipper! Chipper! And no, our call doesn't mean the word
in English but that it connects with you in that way is a good
thing.

Cheer is a good thing!

And you know if you listen there is much else we say.

We are not a repetitive kind of bird. We have lots of calls
and lots of things to say and we are BEAUTIFUL! and we are
BRIGHT! and we are RED! We are RED!

And we are very capable birds. We are just the right size. We
can do anything we want.

We are not prey for just anything that comes along. We are not
so big that we can't enjoy ourselves.

We love life. There's lots to eat. There's sunshine and then rain
and then when the rain stops and the sun comes out, that's a
very good time.

Sometimes you know we're just calling one another to say Look,
there's food here! Sometimes we're calling to say Mama! Papa!
— just calling to check in and see where everybody is and what's
going on.

You're right to be in love with us. We are ... oh, it's a very good
kind of bird to be. We are so capable and we have a great range
of interests and things that we do. And especially are we not a
good color?

CROW AND BLUE JAY

I am your Crow! And I am waiting to talk with you!

And I am your Blue Jay! And I am waiting to talk with you! Because we have been at your side all your life.

I Crow fly back and forth between darkness and light. I know what light of darkness is. I know the sacred laws that keep order. I shine.

You have a word, *brave* — in the old days, meant fancy, handsome, beautiful... bright. That's me.

Look at the light on my wing. Nothing could be darker. And nothing could be lighter.

Yes! You are right about how I shapeshift. *By containing all the shapes within me.* Containing everything! And knowing Who I Am, and then saying *Yes!*

And I, I am Blue Jay! I am your totem. And I am sky-magical blue feather and word. I am Word. And you are magical in word. And that's what I am holding for you and always have.

I too fly back and forth. I fly back and forth between sky...and sky! Ha! I am a flash of sky!

Nothing fancy! But nothing could be brighter than the BLUE of my wing and the light shining from my wing and the light in my eye!

And you, my little jay one! You can get lost trying to figure things out. So don't. Just take it from me! Just get in touch and talk. Hahaha! I'm a wordslinger and so are you.

Keep me with you. Keep me with you. I'm quite at home, and Crow too is quite at home with this channeling business. It's an old story for us!

When you moved into your cabin, who was outside calling to you? Yes! Saying hello! Welcome! This is the place! This is *your place!*

That was a good time for you. Now you live in a place with no jays, and no crows really either. So you must come to us in your imaginary worlds! Come back to your little cabin and speak with us. We're fond of you, our girl. So be it. We've finished. Goodbye.

MAUNA KEA

Because you love the whole of this mountain, love what you call the flanks, and the mamani seeds and colors of the dust, We speak.

We mamani trees, we feel this also. But we are slow speakers.

Bees also, yes, and we are fast speakers!

We are a body, a field, a We. And so are you. We feel the light angling. Moving across. As you feel light of sun moving across your shoulders.

We are *high, high, high...cold, clear, bright...dust, earth, hot, barren... exposed exposed exposed!* Curvature of earth, sky rounding about you. Hard to breathe.

Exposed! Bare light striking all around you. Clear edged, sharp. Sharp shadows that you make.

Light comes in to fill what is exposed. This is what light does. Light makes clear. Light reveals. Light penetrates. Light makes happen.

But that shadow, that filling inward, that flaying off, that revelation, that exposure, that experience is a *human* one.

As for us, We are multitudes. We are flanks, hollows, ridges, roots, risings...softness too, as you know. Softness, colors of dust and grasses, trees, dirt, veldt, beaches of black sand.

I now speak — I, deepest roots, deep below.... *I Am Ancient.* Outer flesh changes, the skin of Me. You see the changing in your time. What was koa forest, now gorse is filling all the space. All will be different.

You love koa. You are saddened by gorse and the end of koa on the mountain. The end of pastures, grasses. All to be gorse. You love the solitude, the silence and the old plants. You grieve.

We say to you, your poem of Us can be a hymn. A hymn to silence — not silencesilence, there are birds, winds, other not-human sounds — but a *peace*.

Let your love for all the places you love be in your poems. Come in love. Come singing your hymns. Come to enjoy, to praise — sun, light, wind, silence, singing, odors — all this is joyful.

We say to you: your body is made of the body of earth. Sensation is your way in. You are welcome here. We speak this.

TORNADO SONG

Sensation of gathering, whirling, greater and greater excitement.

Tornado Tornado TORNADO!

Feel this whirling over below-lands, gathering, drawing color, dust, dirt, sucking up, drawing up into!

Feel this? This is very elating! There is no anger! We just are what we are! We do what we do! Where there are the conditions for reception, then we do what we do.

Humans make the space for reception. Humans know what makes a space for reception of tornadoes and what does not. But humans have other priorities.

It is a pleasure to manifest! It is a pleasure for us to manifest! It is a pleasure for you to manifest! And it is a pleasure for those to manifest who are in places where tornadoes come. And they plow or do what they do, and then the conditions are ripe! And what fruit is plucked is...tornado!

But as for us, we are what we are, just like you. You have seen us gather on the horizon, you have seen us roil across the sky. And it was beautiful and exciting. We are beautiful and exciting. We are movement that has shape and coherence. And that is beautiful.

It feels like manifesting. Like expressing to the call. It feels like becoming! Like being! Like becoming!

HONESTY

Remember what it feels like to be a child. Oh, lose inhibitions, and be a child!

Everyone is so absorbed in all the evils and injustices and turmoils and ugliness and being angry and being sad. That's not your work. But it may be their work.

It's not up to you to tell them. What you can say is, this is *my* work. I am channeling the consciousnesses that choose to speak through me.

Those that wish to speak through you — they come first! Let your integrity stand in alignment with *them*. Stand in what is *true*, which is that they have spoken through you. So don't get off the beam too much in how you present it, trying to make it less difficult for people to accept — trying to hide what you are!

And don't let a positive response from people draw you off too much, either. Rather, take your stance in truth, integrity! Don't settle!

You're not afraid of anything in the wild. Indeed you are in love with all. But in your whole life, you have never let down your guard with a human being.

Now, you must be honest about what you are doing. About who you are. And about who is connected with you and is speaking to and through you.

You must be honest. You must have integrity. Or all the light, all the light will seep out of it!

The time for protective coloring is over. Now is the time to stand forth. Shine very brightly! I am with you. I am with you. I am with you. Hold me in your heart, my jewel between your eyes.

CROW SONG

I am Crow. I am of your kinship, as you have long known, whether you knew it or not.

I am black and shining. I watch with one eye and then the other eye. I am always with you.

Crows have yelled at you and companied you and sung to you and stayed with you through many dark times in your life, and you did not even know it until they were almost over.

We were there in the trees yelling

Wake up! Wake up! Wake up! Wake up! Wake up! Wake up!

And finally you woke up.

We are fond of you. There is an aspect of you that belongs to us. It is a shining darkness. And you have written good poems about us. True poems.

But the light that is in darkness, the gleam and shining in darkness, this is something for you to think about and write about and embrace.

We are sometimes happyhappy and we are sometimes loud and raucous and we do not take any shit from anybody. And you should practice that more.

But also we shine, in the very blackness and gleam of our feathers, the stars, the vast shining of the universe.

We are comfortable with All That Is. *All*. And you can be too. Embrace and love the gleam and shine of darkness. The obsidian light.

Hawk Song

High. Light. Air. We are Hawk. We hunt and we play together. We ride the winds up the bluffs and off and around! And if we see something small far below...we dive!

Riding on open wings — a feather change and soar! soar! The feel of the warm upcurrents!

It is keenness, seeing, diving, catching, eating! It is odorous of all the things you humans cannot much smell. It is brightness, light, sun, sky. But mostly it is the feeling under our wings!

And the shouting! shouting! to one another...and diving and scooping, scooping! It is good it is good it is good!

I have nothing more to tell you. All humans, they are storytelling, they are making something *coded* from us — but that is not our experience.

Some like whales and dolphins and crows and blue jays have things to say to you. But we hawks do not have a mythological component, not to ourselves.

To ourselves...we fly! we soar! we feel the muscles from inside! We are pleased, we are pleased!

And we play with one another around and around and riding on these good currents of air up and over the bluffs....

And down below very small thing moving, but we do not miss it we see it! We see it! We get it!

Goddess at Ghost Ranch

Immensity of light. Blueness like a bowl above. Orange, and dusty green, and golden dust. And silence. In which small small small movements and voices can be discerned.

Everything going about its life. And you can be here, a presence that does not deform the field. All here takes you in, and begins to harmonize you into the song.

You smell the smells of dry. Of sage. Of dust. Of gray green plants, bushes that don't need much water. Tough-leafed. Prickly.

In the river bed the red-orange soil is damp. Tree-thickets overhang. Water below the earth. Here in the creek bed it is damp red-orange clay.

Remember this. You are making a shape of river clay with your hands. You make your goddess shape — not a named articulated storied goddess, but All That Is, though you do not know that yet.

All That Is, including you, is the power, the light, the creative pour — and the opening, the shaping. She is the possibility of shape. The continual changing chalice of presence.

The saying: I am open to receive. I am open to receive. I am open to receive. I am open to receive. I am open to receive.

This is the water path. Remember.

BEAR

I Bear am often in your poems.

You have a connection with me, especially when I go deep into the cave and sleep, and there bear my young.

The seed sprouts. What is dreamed comes to life. In silence, clarification, solitude, the cave and the light in the cave.

I am also much of your kindred in the autumn — the autumn of life as well, where you are now. In enjoyment of the riches of the earth. Pleasure in sunlight, in taste and warmth and gleaning all the wild flavors and colors and lights and odors of autumn.

And there is a fat time when the salmon run. And we glut when glut is to be had and it is beautiful. The clear high bright cold warm sky. The immensity of the surface of earth. The fast waters gleaming and glancing and sparkling and making a rushing noise.

And the salmon filling the waters. Spawning. Dying. It is a great thing that happens. Many die. Many die. And many are born from the spurting of seed and floating in the water are vast networks of life to come.

It is dying and living on the same ground, in the same field.

And we eat.

And in our own cycles we come from the cave in the early spring and we eat what we can find. We nurture our young. We teach our babies. We love our babies and care for them. And they forth and we forth.

And it is possible that the time is coming for a killing ground for us as well, and that the seed will not bear, in this dimension. The seed will not bear, the killing ground will be for us, in this dimension.

But we would say to you, there are many doors from the cave. There are many dimensions. There are many Bears. It is like a dream and waking to a different place. There are many dimensions.

EXPANSION

THE TARN IN THE SIERRAS

I am Rock. Snow, soft on me, melts and I hold a water....

You came. I remember you. Body in water, on me sprawled.

I communicate in vibration. Off-giving, in-taking. Very slow. Slower than trees. We know when trees are within us: their vibrations. We are cognizant. But very big. Very slow.

All is in good order. You little rushing small things, you hurry into the world and out of the world so many times. And we come in and out very slowly. We are cognizant of things much changing.

We contain. And we integrate slowly. We contain a water for you, a drinking for birds, and a small mammal, and ants. And below, waters for trees.

And deeper down down down — fast creeks fastcreeks fastcreeks fastcreeks! That makes a sound, a vibration. It is a vibration that you are particularly drawn to. It is a quick sound. Quickwater. It is a bright happy musical sound.

You have an affinity with water in this form. And with lakes, water held in granite. Yes. Because it is clear water. It is light through water. You have a particular affinity with clear bright water. Creeks. Fast small rivers.

And with shining granite rock. It is rock. You think of it as bones. And this is all right. It is a metaphor.

Up here you are exposed to air air air air air light light light light light. Nothing between you and rock. Nothing between you and light.

This is what you have affinity with. Clarity. The thing in itself. We say to you: *this* is your poem. The bone, the rock, the bone, the air, the light, the fast clear water, all exposed, all clear, all exposed.

Write. Write this. Write this. Elation. Expansion. Terrible joy. Light that Is. That IS.

Here on top of this mountain we speak of Truth. *Truth!*

The rock of things. The clear pure air. Light. *Knowing.* Without padding. Without padding.

Expose yourself. Expose your poems.

Do it. Do it. Do it.

Relax!

The channeling of the granite tarn mountain was a very powerful opening. And always when there is an expansion there is a brief contraction from that. Because it is exposed. And it is new. There is a part of you that is trying to protect you from the unknown.

To be exposed and asked to be more and more and more exposed! That was a call! But also a hugely exhausting and demanding call.

So we say, experience the relaxation and pleasure and fun of just being in a place you enjoy, in nature, in your imagination.

Channel with us faeries in these places! Lie in the grass in the sun and listen to the birds and the bees and to the small singing of us as we enjoy and tend to what is there by enjoying and appreciating it!

This will give you some love experience! Of not worrying, of not seeing an enemy all the time and standing forth to protect. You can relax and say to yourself many times a day — maybe many times an hour! — maybe this is your mantra! — *All is well. All is well. All is well.*

All That Is is so much vaster and more powerful than you are allowing yourself to imagine and experience. And your own power is not the only power there is! That sounds silly but that's what you've been acting from!

So let it go, let it go. All That Is is All That Is, and expressions are just expressions. And nothing is changed by putting your fat finger in! Allow everything to become in each moment as it will.

Hear that sound of *you?* Like a gong striking? *Your* gong over and over and over saying *I am This. This. This.* This is the path.

SIERRA MEADOW AND FAERIES

The Sierra meadow in early spring. A creek running through. Snow banks all around. Everything is so green and the water is so clear and sparkling. Little flowers all through the meadow. The sound of the creek. Atwitter with birds, the whole air! Birds talking. And the creek talking. And the sun high up above in a blue blue blue sky.

Hello! Hello! Yes, we know you, you know us.

In your beginning time you were open to receive us. And we would say, "See! See! See! Smell! Smell this! Listen! Hear this hear this hear this!" And you did!

There's no difference between love and joy! Not to us! Love and joy, joy and love.

And dancing! Dancing for joy. Singing for joy! And loving. Feel that? Feel your heart? Yes!

Just being! Just being. Just being. Feel the sun. Languor and pleasure. All your limbs relaxing in pleasure. In the sun. And your ears full of birds.

And us! Us! We are many kinds of beings here. Our realm is not a different realm. It is right here. It is the same.

It is the same place, but a sliding. An overlay. An underlay.

We are in love with all this. And you — you be in love too!

Sovereignty

As we have said, you do not have to behave a certain way to earn our love or be part of us. You are part of us.

We are the closest in affinity to you, and so we are your family of light. And we are different from your family on earth in that our knowing of you is of your wholeness, of all that you are.

And in that our love is without judgment or conditions. For how could there be? There are none in actuality. They don't exist.

Similarly if you were in your wholeness perceiving another in its wholeness, there would be no judgment. And there would be perception of and respect for sovereignty.

You would perceive each person, animal, being, each unique multidimensional wholeness as sovereign — as powerfully flowing into its current experiencing self, powerfully manifesting its own life.

It would not occur to you to change, fix, correct that — it would clearly be manifesting as it chooses to manifest! In order to experience!

You would respect that sovereignty. And the same is true of yourself.

WHAT TO TRUST

What can you trust in making decisions? Well, you have come to trust in who you truly are. And in the love of your family of light. You feel unconditional love from the Divine Mother. So already where you feel trust is in the expanded multidimensional actuality. Including *your* wholeness as well as *Oneness*, All That Is.

And you trust the nonhuman world, where there is complete unconditionality and living in actuality, which is the source of your deep restoration in nature.

It is easy for you to be multidimensionally conscious and to channel. And that gives you a sense of trust. You feel it when you are there: Oh, this is my natural state. I belong here, doing this. And that's a source of increasing trust in who you are.

And it is also true of your nature as a poet. Putting aside all the issues that are transactional, turn your awareness to the nature of *you* — the nature of *you* includes this natural flow of poetry. This is who you are. And this you can trust.

All your experiences in multidimensional actuality feel trustworthy, reliable. All reinforce your *knowing*...because actuality is actuality is actuality.

And knowing how things actually work will gradually help inactivate some of those old patterns that are transactional, wherever they came from — and our suggestion is not to be the key-hunter but just let the plants and grasses grow right over those.

To know what the right thing is to do, ask yourself: what should I do next — this? or this? You can feel the difference. If you are disconnected from your wholeness and from actuality, that is when the window gets very foggy. You don't know what to do, you don't know what you want, because you can't hear *yourself*.

HUMAN EXPERIENCE

Expand, expand, expand...relax and expand. Sunlight is coming through your eyelids. You are permeable to light even in this body — you know this but you don't know this.

Feel light within, throughout. Within, around, and through you is light. And light has infinite colorations to your human eyes and imagination. Gold now coming, gold coming, gold of sun and warmth and expansion.

And the particles that make your body are vibrating faster, and the space that makes your body is expanding.

Now you can perceive yourself as a cloud of particles. Expanding and vibrating, vibrating more and more quickly, higher and higher frequency.And the light can be any coloration you wish, but right now it is pouring in gold.

In human body life, this kind of experience is difficult to realize because of the tightness and fear, and all the ideas. So all of one's energy is in *thinking*.

The lightness, the vibrating actuality, the cloud of particles, the light within and through and around and beyond that — this is limited by imaginary separations.

In truth all can merge. And that merging feels blissful. Humans have experienced a merging in sexuality or in loving feelings for another or in beautiful, poignant music or poetry, or in dancing, running, sweating, doing things with the body. But normally it is not easy.

Even those for whom it is easier don't have a structure for it, because it is not something that human thinking allows for. So they are called "sensitives" rather than it being recognized that in fact this is just how it is.

There is no human intellectual structure for oneness. Or for merging with oneness, or with other kinds of consciousnesses. There is no intellectual structure for the primacy of consciousness.

So humans experience through limiting assumptions and ideas: that there are two separate realms, natural and supernatural, that only the physical world is real, that consciousness is an artifact of the physical and so forth. And this is fine! This is how humans play — through polarities!

Self Loving Self

You are a delight. So fluid and such subtlety and coloration of light! From very very bright and sunny and joyous and intense, to dreamy and light just coming over the horizon... and all the music that you make in all your moods. These moods that you think of as a *problem*.

The only thing that gets in your way, darling, is that mind in chains. The old chains. Slip out! And in every possible way you are Us! embodied.

Embodied, and so radiant with All That You Are! So the most beautiful thing you can do is just intensify your knowing who you are. Knowing and loving as we do.

No — loving as *you* do! As I your infinite Self loving *myself!* Experiencing life through this embodied self — as though your skin and body are irradiated!

I/We/You are very very beautiful. And we think that the greatest gift you can give yourself is embracing this knowing of who you are.

If you are truly in love with yourself — your infinite Self and your embodied self too — if you are in love with this radiant expression, there is so much to be experienced! So much to be known/loved in the world!

This is the greatest gift you can give to your channeling practice — loving, loving, loving, loving, loving all that arises. Beginning with yourself.

Allow yourself to practice this. Come within and feel this flow of colors and light qualities and emotions and moods and feelings and sounds and the pouring of the immensity of you in that rushing wave of the ocean of you. In that pouring, bubbling, clear, bright colored river of you!

There is so much movement and light. That's something for you to speak, to word! — that *sensation* of love, of us loving our darling.

Share in your *own* love — your own vast wholeness loving this fluid expression, this moving changing bright soft manycolored radiant ocean of light, river of light. We sing with you, we sing to you, we rock you in our never failing love. For it is *you*, it is *I/you/we* ... my own wholeness loving my own girl.

Space Within

Expand inward. Rather than open your face and head as if to something from outside, try to feel from inside — heart, throat, solar plexus. The back of the heart also.

Feel yourself expand from this cave *inward* into *vastness*. Within you is all this space! Dark, and lit with so many suns and stars.

Feel this expansion! Come down into this. Let your head go. Bring consciousness down into *this*!

All harmonizing. All singing. This *Is*. This is *infinite*.... *Space....* *Space.... Space.... Light....* Billions, trillions of light!

Sparks. Flashings. All very clear white light. Sparks!

Remember this when you begin to think of earth in polarities. This *IS*.

Earth is this also. Earth is vastness. Sparks of light within. Many many many earths. Many many many lives! Life = Spark! Remember this.

What is playing out in the minds of humans, it is just play. It is a little volcano spurting and hissing. It's very exciting.

But step back, step back, and in the vastness of All That Is, and in your own vastness, experience.... Space.... Sparks.... Music .... Many flows of light....

You can zoom in and out, in and out. When you zoom in, life is a pouring in, a flow of light, all colors. And when you zoom out it is a spark. It is a sparkle in darkness.

Singers from Far Away

.... You are thinking of all the ones you know of. Let that go. We are not from the "usual places."

We are very beautiful...very distant. We are coherent light, connected. It is not like anything human beings can imagine, we think.

We are embodied, though very differently from you. When you are aware of harmonizing energetically — that harmonizing, if you can be in that, you have a close experience to our way of being.

It is difficult to talk about it, because though you are trying to think differently, you still think as humans do, and this is by *distinction* of one thing from another.

The way we experience, and communicate — the way we *are* — is like your Oneness and how you, as consciousness within that, are unique and yet not separate. This is as close as we can come to giving you an understanding.

We experience light directly. It is like the experience of *expansion* — that is the best way we can describe it in a way that you have experienced. The in-you-physical experience of expanding, can you feel that? That is your embodied being's experience of light coming in.

We are not giving you what we would like to give you, but approximation. We would like to express for you the flexibility and speakingness and articulation and quickness of communication by direct experience of light.

Light speech for us is slow and sweeping and graduated and there is much subtlety. It would seem to you, we imagine, like one note, but it is not one note.

We have a connection with some on earth. But unlike some star systems that are very connected and involved in the expansion of earth and interested in human beings, we are not very interested in human beings.

We are interested in you because in your essence you are connected with us. And the detachment you worry about in yourself is an expression of this aspect of light that we share with you, and with many that are not human, and with some other humans.

With you as you grow older there is happening a natural clarification, becoming lighter, becoming clearer and higher frequency, and more detached.

When you were a child you were like us in a child way, you were like our — we do not have children in the way you have children, but our beginning time. What is interesting is that as you grow older in this embodiment, you have refined more and more and more into this aspect of your essence which is very attuned to ours.

So we are not here to help you or give you advice. We are not interested in human lives. But we are interested in singing with you, if you tune to us! You can call and sing with us.

And we do not only mean a metaphor for your harmonizing with other consciousnesses. We say, sing with your vocal chords! Tune to us! That we *will* do with you! That we *will* channel. That we will channel. That we will channel.

We do not love, but we bow to you.

Jophiel says: It is like the many many different strands of your DNA, and one of your strands is this. You have a strand that vibrates with this field, let's call it that, like a strand vibrating on a stringed instrument although that is not literally true.

We are very excited for you about this! An aspect of your field is being brought out by that vibratory affinity and their recognition and response to that affinity. It is bringing out that aspect of your...let's call it your song.

Love Is Creative

To love unconditionally is to know and appreciate the nature of something, to align with and open your heart to that way of being. And thus you create more of what you love.

So it is through love that you, Ruth, create a poem.

Love for another being is your awareness of their unique "who they are"-ness, the fullness of their being. Your aligning with and true seeing of that is love.

But to be unconditional with the world around you does not mean having to accept everything! You are mistaking unconditionality for not being able to choose!

These are different things. It is absolutely possible to turn away, un-align, from what is undesirable to you!

It is unconditionally being present.

Unconditionality is the way in which things actually exist.

Choosing what gives you joy is creating your life through love.

INFINITE SPACE

Expand.... Expand...into the whole universe, all the universes! Sparks, sparks...everywhere sparks of light, stars!

We speak to you and we are *vast*! And the more you are your vast wholeness, the more we can connect! The more *we* are All That Is and the more *you* are All That Is and the more merged All That Is in All That Is, then it is so easy!

All the lights in each resonance, each version of your earth, are all like stars. Flowers, trees, human lives, all are lights. There is, you see, vast space within each, and within All That Is.

Now you know that universes are both *within* consciousness and *are* consciousness. And consciousnesses are quicksparks! that expand, *Whoosh!* into Oneness!

And Oneness is *in* quickspark...and *is* quickspark! *Life = Quickspark!* And ... *whooosh!* again! Wave to particle to wave to particle to wave .... This is how it is, how it works!

What you are translating is the All That Is speaking. And your own vast wholeness speaking. So it is less personified now. It's always been a merged field for you, but merged in a much more personal way, yes?

Even the word merge is not right, is it. It's interflowing space and light and...*quickspark!* Vast *expansion!* Vast! Every quickspark! Every quickspark is immense! Immense!

Cultivate this capacity to experience as nonphysical. You will find it is also easy for you to go into the space within your body. *Space is a kind of consciousness.*

The nonphysical, the space, the knowing that lights, consciousnesses, sparks are each a *universe* — this parallel of life with cosmology, galaxies, universes — this you can contemplate.

Life Is for Fun

Ahhhhh! Wheee! Riding the light. Can you imagine that? Riding the light!

Like a rainbow that you're riding with your body! *Whoosh* and *whoosh* and *whoosh*!

We are less interested in speaking to you in words. We want you to experience expansiveness as you did the other day, this time experiencing light, colorations, rainbow-ism.... All the infinite colors.

What you see is so narrow a band, but there are infinite colors! And infinite gradations of lightness and lightedness and fullness of light of brightness brightness!

Aha! The light is giving you shivers. Shivers of expansion! This is a good thing. It's good for you to feel this in your whole body.

Now just come back, come back... in.... in.... in... feel *allll* of the back. Unzip the back and step out. You *expand*! *This*!

And you see, it's not darkness you go into today, it's light! It's light! This is fun! We want you to turn more to fun!

Life is for fun. For fun! For fun, interesting, pleasurable, expansive — to feel, to know, to get it, to create — all of that!

It doesn't have to be "fun" in a limited way. These vast unlimited experiences you have with us? Fast moving and bright and light, light! That is fun. Expansiveness and fast movingness!

FIELDS OF AFFINITY

We are all fields, and you are merged with us when you channel. When you expand, you experience Oneness very flowing in and out of itself. It is much void and therefore much, much Oneness. It is only when a "someone" compresses and becomes tight and small, that nothing can get in.

The more space, void, the more merged Oneness. And within Oneness there are all the unique and beautiful ways of being. Various fields. Consciousnesses pouring in and out and in and out. The darkness of space space space, with the sparking in and out. And within your own body field also, void *is*, void is.

We now speaking — the field "Alayah" — are not "you" in the way that your own wholeness speaking is you, but more like your "almost twin" in the nonphysical. It is not this exactly, but in human words.

And the Divine Mother field is a mother-ness. Not a person of the stories. Because all your life you called to motherness, and thus motherness is always here for you. "Mother Mary" and "Divine Mother" are human constructs around motherness. Motherness was another aspect of human experience that you chose, when you came in, to experience in a distorted way, although by "distorted" we mean only to describe.

For unstinted from its clear path, the flow of mother-ness flows in one direction. But when there is great need for motherness upstream, this asks that flow to come upstream. And so you were asked in your child body self, and through much of your life, to *give* motherness. This is a metaphor.

Light is neutral. It touches, is fully present, perceives, loves, and moves on. And this pattern, which is who you naturally are, is not within the human approval patterns. You are late in life coming to love who you actually are, coming to feel less guilt and shame and badness for being what you naturally are. We remind you that from our perspective there is nothing wrong in your natural state.

Other energies also are in your fields of affinity, which you think of as your family of light, and this is the way perhaps to best think of them, as energies.

Energies of your joy-singingness Singers, your bright, bright, bright Dragons, your joyplaying Dolphins. The energy of pure unconditional love of you, which Duffy brings concreteness of. And others. All these energies are here for you and speak as you call upon us to speak.

We remind you that angels also are not as pictured and conventionally experienced! Field called Jophiel is gold, clarity, integrity, truth, pure light! *Be true! Be true! Be true!* And Ariel field is energy of love *BeHereThis*. Love here, now. Love all this that is! Love Now Now, *This This This*.

We are fields of energy, vortexes within All That Is. We are All, we are all We, and we are all You.

PLACES AND VOICES

REDWOODS

Be aware that you are actually aware! Channeling is not always the formal speaking in words. Channeling can be connection all your day and night.

Just breathing — your respiration and our respiration. This is a joining. We breathe into one another.

We hold light, sun inside. In our bark, but further in, sunlight running through our veins. And we breathing you and you breathing us, this is — can you feel? — a harmonizing. As you know the harmonizing that is like music, that is like dawn color, now know the harmonizing of breathing, that is like rhythm. That is like joining. And is also the pulse of becoming.

Though your flashing in and out is so much quicker, it is also a pulse — from wave to particle to wave to particle. Becoming. Becoming. Becoming. And we suggest that you practice breathing with us. In this way becoming, becoming, becoming.

Now around you is the deep grace. And the fluid multidimensional consciousness, the fluid in-and-out becoming becoming becoming of trees and all the other lives all around.

All the little quicknesses, the sparklings — the birds and the light and the old mosses, the old hanging lichens, the deep broad slow beings of trees. And the small quick beings who love and tend these trees.

So we say now: just breathe and be here, without words. There is plenty of time, day and night, asleep and awake, all the while that you are here. We wish you to rest and be conscious sometimes without words. Allow yourself to be present, and to relax into this presentness. All is manifesting here, as you are. A vast multitudinous field of which you are part, with no thinking beyond that.

Slow down. Let us take care of things. Just rest and be happy. Be less hard on yourself. Relax. It would be good for you to know you can open your back and lean against what *Is*. Try it: open your back and lean against the becoming that includes you. The love, the unconditional awareness that includes you.

We suggest that you let this time be a learning of new ways that are supportive and multidimensional — treedimensional! faerie-dimensional!

For it is a new way of thinking for you to know that all around you is safe, supportive, loving. That you can lean on what is around you.

All your life, who you have been in your body and how you have experienced, it has been in the assumption that what is around you will harm or use or need something from you, or exploit you, or in some way be a demand or a difficulty. There was good reason for this assumption, we know.

But now try what it is like to experience opening all the pores of yourself and feeling unconditional love, wisdom, help, support all around you. Try this. It is a new way of thinking for you, to know and feel that all around you is safe, supportive, loving — that you can lean on what is around you.

You have been brave. But now it is time not to gird your loins so much! To know that we are here.

Pines at Sea Ranch

We express in scent, oil, needle aromatic. And also a sound which you are not hearing now, storm sound. We sough and sough and sough. And that is of us.

These architectures of space which you metaphor like arches of a cathedral and also we remind you, your vision of whale bones. And this also expresses of us.

And dancing. Our dancing is difficult for you to comprehend because you are too fast. Dancing is not imaginable for you so slow.

Imagine dancing when every gesture, every articulation of the dance is perhaps weeks, perhaps moons...always longer than your attention span, little human.

We are dancing with the light, the wind, the air, the ocean sounding, which you can hear now. And the seasons, the heat, the cold, the insects.

And so much of us is happening also invisibly under your feet. You know this is true, but you cannot experience it.

When you slow down like this, then we have something to say and you have something to know, to word. And so this is a thing that happens. A moment.

It is not a pleasure or a not pleasure. It is the thing that it is. It is interesting. It is interesting for you to pay attention and it is interesting for us to feel you here.

In the Sea Ranch Garden

We are here! We are *here* and we are *now* and we are *present* and we are *having fun!*

Feel this beautiful golden light on your body! Feel this beautiful warmth! And even humans can smell this reek of herbs and all these subtle colors!

We too love the sound of the ocean and the wind from the ocean — although sometimes it is too strong, we have to go into cover.

And there are relatives of us who live in the ocean, yes! But not mermaids. You are remembering a full moon night, a night for magic in the glitter and clear on the beach — that was a lovely thing. And the great shy deer that evening.

We are garden faeries. You can sometimes see us, little lights — we sometimes catch the light, is what it is.

So that's enough talk. We really don't like to do talking. We are impatient to be silent and singing in the Now. It is boring what you are doing.

Come! Be with us! You do have a connection, from when you were a child. To open your eyes and be enjoying and loving these plants and what is around you, this is a good way to be in connection with us — not closing your eyes and trying to have us talk to you!

Here is this place! Here is this place! Here is this moment! Here is this breeze, just as it is!

Sometimes you are annoying.

LAPAHOEHOE SONG

Lapahoehoe! Isn't that a beautiful sound? It sounds like the sound of the ocean here, though that's not what it means.

I am a holding place. Soft. Just the right amount of ocean and of earth, in a pattern that is beautiful and soft and pleasurable.

It's pleasurable to be pleasurable! That's what I say. Many enjoy here. Many humans. Many birds. Many plants. Many sea creatures. Many rocks are happy here — long, long rock lives.

Trees also are slow and long. Trees are good for you and rocks are good for you! And people fishing. Because you hurry too much. Here is good, slow, it slows you down. And hearing birds!

There's much going on on this island. New land coming forth the way land comes forth. Comes forth in fire, comes forth rolling through rock, through ocean. We like that the bacteria and the bacteria eaters at the bottom of the ocean are the same with whale fall as they are with the coming of new land.

We are many voices, many are speaking with you! Some are the light beings of this place, small bright spirits. However you need not fear the dark!

In truth you need not fear any of it! But what we are trying to say is, there is a rich burnished darkness that is of light, and that is very nourishing place for you. Think of that as your cave.

You are called to love all — All That Is within you and All That Is around you and All That Is. This is a work in progress.

Very Fast Energies and the Banyan Speak

Hello! HaHA! See, you thought it was going to be serious! But feel this, feel this — what expansiveness is! It's fun! Feel? Wheeee!

We/Wheee (joke hahaha!) enjoy this! This is harmonizing of your vibration with all that is present, at this level, now, together!

We are a very very very fast expansive spacious speaking of words. We are not an identifiable, characterized one, that's not it! This is vastness and *fastness*! Hahahaha!

And so so so much, such light, such light-ness, such clear, such clear-ness, such light/clear/ness! All, everywhere! Lightness, clarity, has words you can speak!

Because this is who you are! This! This! The lightness of you in your ordinary embodied lifetime gives you the hint. This is who you are. Like singing, because it's all harmonized. Like a rainbow, but not in bands. Your wholeness, and our wholeness, and All That Is, is *This*.

You can be *This*. Or you can be more specific. You can be more you-specific, and you can be more anything-specific. And you can word this!

Here's a banyan tree now. Banyan is very huge, distant, under earth. Banyan is speaking all banyans. Here. Now. And sloooow.

There's a juice that is slow. A reaching. A leaning. A reaching. A connecting. A *huge* song — it's all the roots and all the aerials of all the earth.

Through the whole earth, we are one banyan. You humans are so quick. Too quick to connect. But in this state that you are now, we can touch you more.

It's not slow. But even though it's very very fast, it's present forever. No, those aren't the words. There's no Where of it. No When. It's a state. And the state is HereNowThis.

LUCKY THE HORSE AND BODY LANGUAGE OF AIR

Here is this place, this air, the smells of this particular time, and I Lucky am merged too with this.

It's the wind here now. Wind coming across much land. And smell of grass. New grass. And it goes forever. We can run forever.

And we, we, we enjoy this sun. It was hard in winter with ice and snow but now, now is best time! All of us around all of us.

And there is more here than horse. We are cloud and cloud shadow moving and we are all the growings, all colors, smells. We are smells. It is much space here. Water too here. Fast, quick water.

I Lucky am not wanting to talk. I am liking the wind and the moving and the wind blows the bugs away. But I am not joy in having you or anyone on my back! Yes, it is a bonding when a horse and a person know one another for a long time, but that is a different thing.

But I am a good horse. I do my job. And I take it easy. I like the walking, I like the wind, I like getting out of the bugs, that's mostly what I like. Nothing is too important. I don't dislike you. And I don't love you. I like the horses. I'm a good horse. That's all I have to say.

Now We speak. We are this place. Big light! Big light big light all-sky light. It is different from where you live, where light comes *under* and from a particular place. Here, All Sky Light!

All very much space. Very much air. Very much light. You too are much air and much light and we are much air and much light. You feel free here. You feel the air, you feel the breathing of wind through you.

The vast winds, and distances, and movements, this is the speaking of air. Pay attention to the speaking of air now. On your face, around you. It is the body language of air! It is made

up of wind, direction, heat, cool, closeness to earth, closeness
to cloud, and how much space! How much space! And coming
from a long way or coming from a short way and turning
and circling or eddying or long breathings. This is the body
language of air! Now you know!

Pine Trees at Rockvale

Slow down now. Slow down and sit and breathe. Open your eyes to what is around you! Be in love, be here.... *Yes.*

We are a grove. This is a word that we like. *Grove. Grove. Grove.* It›s a slower word. And this slow respiration *groves* us and you with us.

And in the background the showingoff happysong mockingbird — not showing off, *throwing the gold of song* into the air for all to enjoy.

This is what he does, for no reason but to have fun! Here it is, over and over, Ruth, what you are translating, and that is: *All is for no reason. It is for pleasure. It is for itself knowing itself!*

Just throw the gold. Just sing for pleasure, for pure joy.

You have been purposed so much all your life. You have been so earnest! But we say, Fire *enjoys* fire. Snow *enjoys* snow. Rock *enjoys* rock. Wind *enjoys* wind. Storm *enjoys* storm. Bird *enjoys* bird. All, in body and not in body, enjoy Being.

This is not a lesson, Ruth, you already know this. It is a practice.

MOCKINGBIRD

Yes.I.Am! I am shiny! I am rainbows! I am making rainbows of sound in the air. Can you hear that?

Oh, I understand you are a singer too, but not the same way I am. I *sing*. I sing many, many, many, many, many, many. If I hear, I can sing.

For you it's different. For you it is — you merge with it, merge with it and speak it. This is different.

If you made a sound, I could do it. I am sheering light of sound. I am rainbows of sound. I am flung flung song through the air. Seeds! I am seeds of song.

Yes, yes, yes! I am magical bird. Many of us are magical. Many of us are magical. But I am the premier singer, I am!

This is a good place for me because I bring that energy and hold that energy for all who come here. So there is energy of the house which is calming and centering and mothering, and there is energy of me, which is bright seeds of many songs. We work together. It is a good place.

We pines also sing, as you know. Wind-singing. Wind-singing. And under the earth ongoing many songs of us. And resinous songs in the sun. Yes.

And now in the distance you hear the train and that too is a song from far away. And the wind rising. Wind would not have a song now if it were not harmonizing with us. Playing, symphonizing.

We suggest for you, breathing. Just breathing. Just breathing And in the wind, on the air, on the breeze, is this odor of pine, which you love. It is volatile. It is volatile and airborne and so can you be — volatile and airborne. Odorous, oh, odorous of All That Is.

'OHI'A

I am a star being. I share with you a detachment that comes from being connected with other stars, a lightness of spirit and a physical fluidity.

I am here to show the way of being connected with your wholeness and being unconditional.

What is most akin in us is this detachment and being more aligned with the wholeness of our Selves, and knowing that we are in harmony with All That Is, and practicing the flexible fluid light, and enjoying enjoyment.

Enjoying enjoyment! It is a different thing from human values and it is what I want to encourage you in, enjoying your own enjoyment!

To expand your attunement both to the stars and to your own wholeness — to resonate with you when you are in alignment and living from wholeness — this is why I have chosen you.

I am also dark light, the richness of dark light. The richness of woods and colors in shadow — I am a forest creature also.

I am a gift. I have come as a gift to you. There is a long tradition of sacred magical practices we share. Mother Sekhmet. Mother Mary. And the connection with the stars.

So for me, embodying now here with you is also to be recognized for Who I Am. Because you have the capability of recognizing me. To be known is a good thing.

Embracing your catness is perhaps a way to think about this issue of your detachment. Some people do not like cats. But many people do. And to think of yourself as a cat who can go fluidly from one expression to another, this is a good way to think about it.

QUICKWATER

I am the quickwater you love. Coming down from far above, filtered through pores in rock. Crystalline! That's a good word.

Water weaves. Weaves with rock and green and air and light — all the elements braided here. And complete.

You in your embodied self are not familiar with completion, with being whole. All in your reality is seeking, seeking. It's unfinished. It's seeking, or opposing, or running away, or opposing, or seeking. It's very busy, very dissatisfied.

Water does not "seek" a path. That is not the correct word. It is a word humans use, but it is not correct. Water *is*. And all the forces *are*, and All That Is *is*. And if there is water and declension and gravity, water flows.

Water follows what *is* — Now, and Now, and Now. It is present, Now, and Now, and Now. And in this way a creek becomes.

It is a path that expresses infinite *Nows*. Nows made up of height, angle, amount of water, weight, obstruction, gravity — so many things. It is *being*, in the physics of this earth. It is not seeking. Do you see the difference?

Being is: *Becoming. Becoming. Becoming.* There is infinite time. You can relax. The only feeling that is authentic is "being here."

Here is something for you to see the difference between seeking and becoming, becoming, becoming: Feel yourself sink a little bit. Now imagine a billion years of sinking. You would not be making your way, finding your way, seeking your way deeper... but you would be deeper than when you started.

This is the way of allowing.

GAIA

I Gaia have *will*, I Am the consciousness of this planetary field. And much that you and other human beings perceive as devastation — as evil, because that is how you think — these things are happening the way all things happen, by the creating of conditions for them to happen.

So many species are dying away and many of them are species that you have an attachment to. Grieving and honoring those species is a work for your poems. The honoring of what is leaving, the saying goodbye. It is the poetry of remembrance and love.

And in All That Is, these species and your love for them and your praise songs for them, exist. Exist! In the Whole. In All That Is. Thus sadness might be transmuted.

Yes, many human beings are making choices to experience certain things, and these choices will make many deaths of humans and other beings. We see that you become angry when you think of this. But from Our point of view, it is just the playing out of choices, and some species go. What these humans are choosing is a way that will remove most of the humans from the planet.

We have no preference! We have no right and wrong, good and bad, and this is very difficult for you to understand. If this is the way that human choices take humanity, then that is the way it will be. Although whether we are opened to by others in this universe or whether we are closed off is another question — because if aggression is the outcome here it must be quarantined.

But one option that might remain lively and lit up for people like you, no matter what the more common, powerful option is, is the option of Light. Joy, love of the things of the earth. Really paying attention, writing about them — even your elegies, clearly and intensely seeing and loving what is, Now.

Sierra Madre Canyon Song

We are a beautiful place to understand heat and light, dessication and odor. The scent of black sage. And there are bears and bobcats. And we are full of birds. For it was raining just a little bit yesterday, and there is a swimming pool down below, and this is good.

Life is very precious here, because it is very fragile. So we say, isn't it beautiful! Precious life in body! Green life, red life, gold life, black bear life, bobcat life, snake life, dog and cat life — and all the little animals and all the plants — everything singing joy! joy! joy! Joy to be in body, this is so delicious!

You, you sing this too! We say, change your spectacles to joy. To joy! Not rose-colored glasses — earth-colored glasses, life-colored glasses! See how delicious. And enjoy!

And I am Tree beside you. I am faster wording than some. For we speak in so many ways — to move with the wind and rain is to sing in movement. And there is speaking in the roots, the electrical and chemical impulses threading and threading....

But we who are pliant and young and juice is quick in our leaves, we can connect with you and you can word from what we say.

Most of the time you are too fast to connect with Tree. It would be good always to slow down. Just slow down and breathe. Respire. You are light and quick, yes, but we only remind you that there are many ways for light to be.

For slow light reveals and is and sings and harmonizes much. Slow light, slow changing. Quickwater and slow water, quick light and slow light. Air quick. Rock slow.

So now you have a quick-and-slow poem. The quick things. The slow things. And this has come to you today in the sunlight.

WHO AM I?

THE SIERRA MEADOW IS WHO YOU ARE

Here is your place again. Everywhere, sparkles! Air, light, water! Branch tips! Flowers! And mountains all around, and a little bit of snow up there, and the blue blue blue sky. The smell of snowmelt, the smell of mountain, the smell of the creek, and the sound of the creek burbling. In the creek, pebbles shining, all different colors.

You have an affinity with rock. And you have an affinity with water — quickwater and still water. And with infinite clear sky of light.

The elements are here specifically in their aspects that are aligned with and resonate with you. Earth, water, air, fire, void. Earth element is rock, granite seamed with white, the face of rock alight with alpenglow. Air element is high altitude snow-smelling air. And above, the great void of blue, of darkness and light. Water element is snowmelt or quickwater or clear stillness of mountain lake. And for fire, the great starfires, and the small sparkles, and the moon!

You have great affinity with starlight — cool, clear, effervescent — the light of truth, clarity. And with the void, darkness soft as 'Ohi'a cat's fur, and stars like cool suns, cooled by distance. This you swim in, expand in, and it is also within you.

This is your homeland — your earth place and your place in the universes and in the void, the sparking in and out and in and out of wave into particle into wave, which humans see as death and birth.

So this mountain place, which you often dream or imagine, is not simply a place of respite. You *are* this place. It is your body; it expresses who you are.

POWER INSIDE THE STEM

We the Dolphins are here! For it is the joy of play that creates! Delighting, delighting, delighting — this *creates*. We the Dolphins say: you focus on this and don't worry about the rest. Just enjoy, play, create!

And We! We the Dragons! say, Yes, it is true that we speak of Power, but your power is *inside, inside*. You come into *your* power! Your power is *inside* the stem of the grass. Your power is *inside* the twig, the branch, the sprig. You are the *juice*.

Your kind of energy is not reaching out and being in the world. There are many, many, many ways to be in one's own power! Your work is of love — attending, knowing from inside — delicately and in gentleness, softness, in silence, in the quiet. Yes.

Others are moving outward into the world now, and are in connection there, but you are moving inward. And that is where your speakings come from — inside the leaf, the dust, the air, the drop of water, the silence.

You go your *own* way. You have said what it is that you want — solitude and nature and quietude to channel and write, to sing! It is good to know what you need to flourish, to water your own plant of you, and choose that first.

To know that you are not another, and that you must serve your best conditions for you, that is truly loving yourself. That is a very good thing. It is a good thing for you to decide where you want to experience — *inside*, inside the leaf, the twig, the drop of water, the lake, the sky, and find a way to go there.

And this *is* power. It is being in integrity with your Self.

Fear of Being Exposed

You feel that you need to run away and hide in order to safely be who you are. But it is time now for you to channel openly. If others do not believe in what you are doing, they do not have to! Permission is not needed. You are who you are. And there is no need to justify yourself. Even if there is hostility and denigration. You have a right to be who you are.

Mystics and hermits had to find a way to crouch within the overbearing structure of the Church. They got permission. Had they not gotten permission, they would have been killed for witches. This is in essence what you fear.

Think about that huge contraption of misunderstanding, into the corners of which those who were in an authentic relationship with All That Is and with themselves and *could not be other than who they are*, had to crouch and pretend!

Your world too is structured by huge contraptions, including the immense contraption of conventional belief that denies who you are and what you experience. But you do not need to crouch and hide or find ways to make it acceptable to others. No one is going to kill you. They are not!

It is time for you to channel as you channel and to translate as truly, poetically, purely, intensely as you can. And this you should do without explication, excuse or hiding. And let the chips fall where they may.

Yes, we understand there was a pattern of being spied upon and that knowledge being used against you cruelly in your previous marriage. But that is over. It's time to be open about who you are.

LIGHT AS POWER

There is a reason you love these high places. You love that feeling of light all around — light light light light! — and air that doesn't feel heavy, air that is dry clear bright-cool. This is your most joyous expressive state. Light flows across the ground, light glimmers and sparkles, light changes, light is not just from one source but from all around, and you are of and in and are light.

This is sovereignty. Understand this. This is sovereignty.

You have habitually associated power with strong emotions of forcing, struggle, *making* it happen. But *light* is power. And light flows. It doesn't have to force.

Feel your lightness in every sense of the word. Weightlessness, brightness, lightheartedness. Light! Light is unrestricted. And although humans create instruments to focus and direct light, in truth light just IS. Not even "all around." It IS. And you are light. So lighten up, ha! about this.

We say, Be in your joy. Be in your joy! There's absolutely no reason to have struggle feelings, fear feelings, worry feelings, anxiety feelings, any of those feelings! Come and play with us! Play with us and just be in the flow of light, the colorations, the "orchestration" of energy frequencies.

There is nothing that can hold onto light. A contraption cannot hold on to pure light. And light moves as it wishes, quickly or slowly and it lights up whatever it rests upon.

Light is "Oh look! Oh look! Oh look!" And light as it touches, *creates.* And that is who you are.

INDIGO AND GOLD

We are coming from very great vastness into your field which has been too thin. Pale dawn-colored light. We remind you that you are also this deep indigo and deep gold. *There is profundity.* There is a profundity capacity, do not forget that. There is deep, profound, dark light. And gold of warmth, joy.

We are storm coloration with gold behind. The blue-violet-indigo is cloudy because it is time for you not to be in your head. It is time for that to quiet. So we are blanketing that now.

And we say, Come into the deepness. Come into feeling and knowing. And trust this. You are too attenuated, too paled. We would like you to come into a deeper knowing of who you are. For you are also this cloudy apprehension that is profound and dark. It is not the clear sparkling darkness you have often experienced. This is like thick indigo clouds, like storm, and behind the storm, gold.

You are being encouraged to experience and speak in colorations, which are less apt to your intellectual pinnings.

We are an expression of the very vast merged field of your wholeness. We are much vaster than we have usually been interacting with you from, because you were not asking for much vaster energies.

I, Jophiel field, am of Oneness, and you are seeing my golden light — both within and behind and roiling with the indigo and violet and dark gray — which is you. Is you! So we are roiling together.

And you see now, there is rose colored light emerging, and deep blue emerging, and many many colors...and yes this is your family in greater wholeness, and you in greater wholeness.

Yet we know you like to feel clarity, so we clear as much as possible the avenues of awareness that are not ratiocination. And you can have a rest from ratiocination. And let the gold roll in like honey.

Listening to Body and Self

Body can tell you what feels optimal, but there is so much momentum in not listening, but rather *telling* body what do, criticizing body, wanting body to be different, that the capacity to listen to the flow of knowledge is lost.

And this is analogous to the blocked flow of one's wholeness into one's life.

There is ideally a flowing into awareness of body knowledge, body preferences — which change — and body optimums. What does your body want? What would feel good now? But much is forced upon body by *thinking*.

Just as ideas, patterns and obsolete beliefs limit the flow of one's wholeness into daily reality.

So if the momentum of not paying attention to either wholeness or body consciousness were dropped and the *Now* were created by your full multidimensional consciousness, listening to your full body consciousness, there would be a very joyful co-creation.

It is very much the same issue in choosing to love yourself. Loving the unique signature frequency of your wholeness is feeling inwardly for that apprehension of *who I am*. Cherishing, nurturing and caring for that is also self-love.

Each body knows what it needs, how it feels best, what weight, what elements, what environment, what movement feels good.

From the moment your wholeness enters the body, body knows and welcomes you. And until the ideas and beliefs and patterns of those around you intervene, it is this pure singing together that creates your life moment by moment. And that is beautiful.

So for each human being, the answers to all these questions about what is right for them come from listening to the body and then giving it what it asks for. And listening to and welcoming the flow of one's wholeness. And nurturing, caring for both of these channels.

Relax and Receive

Expand, expand, expand, open into the darkness, into the vastness alive with lights. Here we are. Here we are again! Here you are again!

Expand, expand, expand. Breathing. You come in and out. It is an analogy. You come in and out.

You can perspective in and out also — into this body...and out.

And now *expand!*...out out out.. . into vastness of space, sparks, sparklings.

Breath fills you. And the meditation that you have used, that the universe is breathing you, is a good one to practice.

The universe is breathing you. And you are breathing the universe.

Just relax and open to receive. What you want, and joy in, and would reassure you and make you feel happy and everything you are asking for, is if you just open like this and receive whatever comes.

Just open to receive. Do this many times a day and see how much better you will feel. You could just relax and open up and ...a flood, a wave coming in, a pouring in of consciousness, a flow, a flow of light, a flow of love, a flow of ease.

Just open up the tap several times a day. That will, we think, give you an idea of how present it is and how little you have to work at it!

Bright Spirit in Chains

There is no magic bullet. This is what you came to experience. If this is to be dissolved, resolved, climbed out of, any of those metaphors, you must do it. All we can do is cheer.

We love you so much and we wish you to be happy. We wish you would choose to be happy be happy be happy be happy; this is the way to dissolve sadness and anger. We do not have another way for you.

You are tired. Try to restore your health, your energy. We suggest that you finish what you have to do and then simplify. And you are on the right path when you say, I don't care if anyone reads my books. Let go, let go of all sadness about that. It is a good thing to let go of all your connections with others for a while.

We love you no matter what. When you're very sad, we say it's okay to be sad, but lifting your spirits and doing what feels fun will help you.You chose this, and there's nothing you chose that you cannot resolve. But you chose to *experience* it.

Understand that part of what you came in to experience was the bright spirit in chains. In chains of culture, ideas, religion embodied in social mores.

The bright spirit in chains, with moments of joy and light and connection — from before birth you were enchained in fear and anxiety and desire to be good, to respond to the loneliness and neediness of others.

This you came to experience. Both the brightness and the chains. Whether you transmute it or not is not the reason you came. You did not come to *fix* it. You came to *experience* it. The whole thing. Who you are and who this chained shape is.

The Realm of Faerie

The realm of faerie has many dimensions, many realms, just as there are many realms of earth. In all places our realms are contiguous with the realms of earth, both the landscapes and the deliciousnesses, the sensory realms of earth, and also the otherdimensional realms that are of affinity with earth.

The realm of faerie is not under the hill! Why would we want to do that? Well, some do, some do. And there are forest faeries and their realm is permeable to forest creatures, and to you when you are in the woods. And there are realms that are meshed with ocean and mist and white caps and foaming onto to the shore and dancing in the moonlight. You saw and thought us mermaids but that is not who we were, dancing there. And caring for, loving the small flowers, there are those of us who are very small and quick.

The human beings with whom you have a long genetic heritage through your father were indeed open to the realm of faerie and connected and spoke with us. I should use not a word that means the past, for it is more accurate to say different frequencies that we slip in and out of. And in a frequency it is always happening.

Your people are of smallness and quickness and awareness, ease in going in, ease in communicating with us and with what is in body and what is not in body. They have been of close working kindred with faeries. But over the centuries, separation, separation, separation.

Also humans have religions. So now Faerie is hidden. And even you do not see with your eyes, though you know we are here, and sometimes you hear and sometimes feel us.

But we are not just here to care for the things of the earth. We are another realm. As animals are another realm — though animals live openly on earth. Yes, there is connection. But not in the simpleminded way that human beings think of it. We are not caretakers. We are living here.

MORE ABOUT FAERIE

Yes, you have been in body in our realm of faerie, and you have been connected with our realm while in body as a human, freely moving back and forth across the barriers. A translator, as you are now. You have had more than one life of passing freely between realms.

There are certainly many silly stories about us! We mean no harm to humans. Humans are a particularly fearful and limitation-held race. And this makes it difficult to deal with them. The real difference between faerie and human is that we know who we are! Humans mostly do not understand why they are on earth — which is to be in joy, to have pleasure, to enjoy being in body and experiencing things and the diversity of the experience.

There is a natural flowing in and out between our realm and the animal realm and the realms of earth elements and growing things. Fast moving water! We too love that sound! And the sound of wind in the trees. We too love the lightning and the thunder. We love the smell of heat in the earth. All that you sense and love, but more! more! Because we have opened the door completely to what is! So for us life is a flowing in and out of bliss and pleasure and joy.

But the things that you humans are obsessed with! Right, wrong, goodness, righteousness, punishment, justice, fairness. All of this is nonsense! The idea of sovereignty does not exist for most humans. And that is why we keep the doors closed. We are pleased that you are seeking to change this and to be open in the broadest sense. And we applaud. But you will notice that most of the time it is only our small quicknesses that will touch and play and be happy and have fun with you physically.

All That Is flows in and out of itself. In an expanded state the realms of faerie and the realms of humans — all the realms of earth and all the realms that are not of earth, in-body and not-in-body — all realms, all frequencies, all dimensions, all fields easily interpenetrate and merge in and out. In an expanded state there is space, space, space! And so the particles of consciousness cohering a realm of faerie can flow in and out of the human realm.

In the All That Is there are no separations. But in the human realm, there are absolutely separations! That's how things are made to work. That's how things make sense!

So in a realm of separation, sometimes little voices or laughter or bells or tapping on your shoulder or sprinkling you with faerie dust...only the smallest of us can ping through. But the realm of faerie is not available because your state, even yours, is not open to it.

There Is No Objective Reality

We say, first of all, that the earth's future is not your responsibility. You know this. And you know that it is most useful for you to love what you love and write about that. This is your role. By saying *This! This! This!* you create more of all you love. That is actually the work.

We understand that you feel that political power and the media have great effect and that there will be, soon, consequences that you do not wish to have be. But in truth there is no time except as a marker. There are many dimensions. There are many realities. In your reality, all these your beloveds live.

So a big idea which you are tied to we ask you to let go of. And this is the idea of objective reality — a shared reality that is objective, that all see or can see. This is not true. *There is no objective reality.* There are only the expressions of consciousnesses. There is consciousness, and the material world is for each an expression of their consciousness.

So this is a very different way of seeing. This is that old bugbear relativism. *There is no objective reality.*

This is not to say that some ideas are not closer to the way it works. Consciousness *is*. And Oneness *is*. And everything is part of the whole, and is expressive of the whole.

Create, create, create your reality and share that. Share that through your writings. Share it through just the vibration of your being. You are a creator. You are not a participant in something that powers greater than you have created. You are the creator of your world. As all are. And to the degree that others allow their worlds to be input from someone else or from the culture, so be it, but you need not.

Begin again to generate a powerful, joyous participation in the consciousnesses of the planet, the elemental life and the tree life and the landscapes and all that is around you. That is a very beautiful reality you create. We want to hear you singing again! We want to hear you channeling the voices, the landscapes, the trees, the birds, the insects.

This is your *making*, you are *expressing this into actuality, into words*. And it's a singing for us. It's a singing for us.

THE ARCTURIANS

We are showing you a kind of flooding of light from a very remote distance. A star system in deep space. Home place for Arcturians. We are connected with you in a valuing of clarity, a valuing of deep space in this universe and of integrity, integrity!

We support you, we sing to you, we resonate with you, in terms of your integrity, your going inward and knowing what is true for you and coming from that, standing on that and speaking truth. *Always* speaking truth. *Always.*

We are a different energy from that of the Dragons who are connected as *charge, charge charge, power, power, power, light, light, light, brightness, brightness, brightness, shine forth, shine forth, shine forth!*

We are *Be in integrity! Speak truth, speak truth, speak truth of who you are – shine forth, but as <u>true</u>!* We send clear white light, and for you the Dragons is a golden light. We are clear white light and very upright, though not rigid.

Clothe yourself in your truth. That word in your language contains your name too, tRuth. This is important – and the metaphor of rue, the English herb of grace, meaning integrity, single mindedness – the turning aside, the letting go, even if painful, of what does not support your integrity.

.

Winter Solstice Restart

Channeling! Poeting! Yes! We are all cheering for you!

We the Dragons, We say, we say! We come forth to help you in this! We help you in flowing light, flowing light, which is *power*! Flowing light, flowing light. We will help. We help! We are here. We ginger you up! Ginger you up! Because we are light. We are bright. We are enthusiastic. We are a kick in the pants. We are a kick in the pants and that's how we help you. We will help you. Yes! We want you to be as uninhibited and bright and flowing the bright light that is you, as We are! Yes!

And We are here also....Yes.... We are...remote. Remote.... You have never sought to sing with us. Ruth. You don't have to be able to sing and you don't have to be able to make the sound we make. We say, try it. Just go inside and invite us to sing with you and your soul will sing with us. Will speak with us. Experience that experience! That will be worth doing.

Darling, of course we are here. We are Jophiel and Divine Mother and Alayah. Spend as much time as you can just feeling who you are. You can feel it and it will give you an experiential of yourself, of the structural, of the signature, of the qualitative nature of yourself.

We have used metaphors of sound, song and coloration and those are good, you can think about those, but in actuality it is a nonsensory apprehension of the structure of your unique field. It is time for you to come to apprehend your *signature*. Perhaps that will be a helpful word for this.

You become tired or stressed and you then turn to consumption of content to keep your mind occupied. When you are tired, dear, just close your eyes and turn everything off and rest. Just rest. Just rest. Ask us for soothing. We suggest that you do this several times a day. Rest your mind, rest your mind. This practice alone will help you reset.

BEING A POET

BEING A POET

Go back, back, back, go back, back, back. Begin again with who you are. With this innate gift of wording. Wording is how you channel, and wording is the poems, the poems like honey.

Like being magical. The poems are magical! And so that is who you are. You are in this wording way, magical, and it is connected with your insight and indwelling, knowing and speaking the consciousnesses of the natural world around you. Your affinity with the natural world and with the stars, the many dimensions and universes.

There is less affinity with human beings. Know that to be valued among humans depends on speaking for and from humans. And you speak, primarily, for and from the nonhuman.

There is nothing wrong with flowing your light, your shining, your joy, your love, and others enjoying it. But that is not the same as the transactional basis of much in your world.

Your need for solitude and being in communication with the natural world is key. The natural world is in perfect harmony with the Whole.

Of course human beings in their interrelations are also part of the Whole — all is part of the Whole! But those interrelations are not what you came in to experience. The experience that is most supportive and creative for you is being in nature apart from human society.

Your way of making words is beautiful — the words and the way of the words, the way of sounding and the music that you make and the meaning and the coalescence of meaning in rhythm and sound and image, all together. We find your writing very beautiful and true. And the truer, the closer to who you truly are.

This is not to say that other ways of being are not part of All That Is. Others have chosen to experience other experiences, and that is part of the whole music. We enjoy the music of multiplicity and diversity. But you are you. Be true to that.

Also you speak the joy of em-BODY-ment. This has always been part of who you are — aware of your own sensory connection with physical life on earth. And this is part of your writing, this joy of being embodied on this earth. Many people are so far from it and that is their choice, but what you can give them is the reminder of this possibility.

There is nothing wrong with enjoying that feeling of creating, expressing, and connecting — having your creative work be transformative, magical, alchemical. There is an "Aha!" when someone reads your words, or when they hear and see and experience through your presence.

There is nothing wrong with wanting to have your work connect with those who are in affinity with it. That is fine! But we say, just release what is finished and let it go. And turn back to doing what gives you joy.

The rest will flow to you, or not. If it does not, so be it. Stay honest. That's all. Stay true to you.

Mountain Top

Here, know what *exposure* means and how exposure has to do with *integrity*. The light, and nothing between yourself and the light, between yourself and the rock. The vast distances and the strong connection with Home.

Over the whole globe, the whole planet, there are these "heads in the light" places. Seeing the whole planet, seeing the curve of globe in all directions curving away from you and the vastness above of space and space and space and space. And your head in the light, in the clouds.

Love all that you love. You could make a huge list. You could make an Ark. All that you love, you can bring into the Ark of your knowing and your speaking. Into your poems. This is a new idea for you.

High above clouds and all the earth turning. And space and the curvature and the light. The light, the light, alight. You are exposed to all that comes from the sun, and to the sun, and then to star light and darkness of space. And light carries you back from the horizons.

The air is cold and cold, and that too simplifies. Your body is wise and your flow from all that you are is wise and there is not so much room in the low oxygen and cold for many thoughts. So it's a good thing to be a little dizzy!

You are practicing now living from wholeness, singlemindedness, astringency, integrity. There's not room for relational things. This compared with that, better or worse than that.

Let your life this year be a growing mastery of the way you wish to live and create. Remember this experience of being up here above the clouds and distant from human beings, exposed to light, headless from dizziness, letting your body and your great knowing speak. Just getting out of the way and letting the wholeness of *you* pour through.

Remember Who You Are

Expand. Experience vastness, space, sparking in and out. Be in this knowing of All that you are, and All that you are in harmony with All That Is. Just breathe yourself out, out, out....

And you see that this is not darkness, it is *space*. It is *void*. It is rest and becoming and *home*. Yes, being in the light is home, but this also is home.

Rest. You will come home. It will be peaceful. And you will be ready. All the work of your hands laid down. And then expanding, expanding, expanding into infinite consciousness, rest, All that you are. Utter consciousness.

Now you are aware of the sparking into being and the returning, and the sparking into being and the returning. Becoming infinite forms, ways of being — even on on earth, infinite ways. Know that nothing is threatened. Nothing comes to harm. All is well. All is expressing, experiencing, returning, knowing, choosing.... Remember this.

It is not that you are doing wrong when you become involved in what is happening in America and the world now and feel strongly right and wrong, anger, grief, fear. It is that you are distracted from your chosen experience and expression — your *work!*

You chose to be receiver and worder, translator and singer and maker of beautiful. It is like the bees making honey, you make honey from the pollen of voices and consciousnesses that are there. It is your path to be open to what wishes to speak in order to express clearly their integrity, their pure truth, the beauty of that pure truth.

And your path is to disentangle from human connections and the emotions having to do with those human ideas. You are not here to teach, Ruth. They will work it out. It is not your job. We say, Remember who you are. Remember who you are.

POETRY AND TRUTH

When you return to the light, you will not experience this complexity. But in embodiment, although your body is in joy of physicality, your embodied self has been conflicted.

Because you chose to be a knower and speaker from *within*, all your life from before birth you have been seeped in human thinking, which is very conflicted, full of ideas that are not in fact the way actuality is. And you have known this thinking *from within*.

And so there is always in you an intrinsic dissonance between what you are experiencing that is the human thinking and feeling — experiencing that as *true*, because you are experiencing it from inside — and the flow of knowing from your infinite self.

This has always been a dissonance and now it is a very great dissonance. You are experiencing this disparity between actual truth and what *felt* like truth for you, which was truth and untruth mixed.

And from that dissonance comes much of the structure of poetry, to hold in tension and not allow either pole to release. And to those who read poetry, including to you, this feels like very profound truth — because like you, they experience this confliction.

So you see that you are in a transition. What you are working on now, these oracles, are not in your terms poetry, not in that old way.

And it is indeed open to you, even while you live in this body, to become more and more truthful, sincere and straightforward and not speak or think or feel from this conflicted place. Or it is possible for you to go on in this conflicted way, and write what you consider, and others consider, finer poems.

And one path is not better than the other, Ruth. If you are focused on making poems before you die that win respect in the human poetry world, that is one path. And if you are focused on *not* feeling and thinking from inside the human, then such poetry is not going to come.

But you might try to speak in another way. We are not saying that it is possible. We are saying that if you want to try, it may be possible to make something beautiful of a different kind of poetry.

Perhaps it might contain both the truth and the human, but in a different way. It might knowingly hold a thing in suspension that you point to, and another thing in suspension that you embody. That might be possible. Embody the light and yet point at a human way or thought.

We do not have an answer for you and we do not say that one path is better than the other. Please keep this in mind. You are not failing if you choose to be a poet-poet, and you will not necessarily succeed if you choose to try to be a Singer who makes poetry, and that is all we will say.

BEING A SINGER

We are the Singers! We sing! We sing! We sing and you sing and all sings together.

All sings! But the active vocalization singing is different from the energetic harmonizing of All That Is with All That Is.

We are *creating forms*. So yes, you are a Singer. Weave in to your song the songs of flowing water, of birds in the trees, of trees soughing in the wind. Of the wind moving, of grasses bending down, and the slow movement of water through the feet of trees.

This is your realm. Your love is most pure and uninhibited where there is the clarity and integrity and truth to self of all these beings and energies.

You are not a singer of the realms of human kind. This you must understand. You are a singer of other realms, but which you bring into sensory realization in the human realm. And that is your work.

You are a *translator* from other realms. Remove yourself inwardly more and more. It is possible to open some connections, and close others.

Both joy and bright sun, and moonlight and water aspects of your nature are in terms of *nonhuman* realms, not human.

Ruth. Ruu..thee...e [*singing*] O, O, O, ah, ah, ah.... You need to practice singing! So you can open your heart and sing with Singers. And the same with those of the other star system who are calling for you to sing with them.

You have a limited idea of singing. And an idea of good and bad in this as in so many things.

Ah, this is interesting! Because sometimes "good" as you use it in speaking of poetry means a sense of what is purest and truest and most perfectly itself. An eagle-like honing in on *truth*, which you call "good." And this is a helpful thing for you in making poems. But this is not what we are referring to.

These faeries and the great Singers, and the Song. You are of the company. Be true to it, Ruth. Be true to the song. And we offer friendship. We here in faerie are very comfortable with all that you are. All the realms are very comfortable with all that you are. And we like you just as you are. Ha!

Breathe in Truth. Breathe out Not-Truth, not any longer Truth. Breathe in Truth. Breathe out Not-Truth. This is a good thing.

I am always with you. I am Black Panther. I am your passion, your intuition, your deep warm shadow. Shadow of Becoming. All you know, all you write, all you speak of darkness is very good.

Darkness darkness darkness. Moon moon moon. Eyes eyes eyes.

Be Who You Are!

We suggest you re-read what, years ago, Stanley Plumly said about you because it is true — joy and happiness and uplift and wit, effervescence, enthusiasm, joy. Don't lose that, he said.

As you let the sediment go down and settle and let the clear pure water rise and the bubbles of effervescence, think of Stanley Plumly's words who *saw* you, right at the beginning of your time as a poet, in *yourself*. This is important to remember.

Be who you are, be who you are, joyous and unafraid of being seen. Just reveal yourself as you are and see wonderful things happen. Trust, trust, trust, have faith, trust. Be happy, be happy!

We love you. We know you. We see you as you do not yet see yourself. You are beautiful. Be in joy. Be in joy.

You came into body to be, in a sense, a magical person and see all the complexities of that and how people respond. And indeed you have experienced this. It is not all roses, is it!

But let go of all those bad experiences now and be fully the magical person that you came in to be. There is nothing you cannot do, so long as it is expressing and in keeping with all that you are.

That's the difference. It's no fun and it's not successful to try to be someone else. Just be *you* and see! You are bright, you are joyous, you are sunshine and we love you.

Returning to Earth

We think it is time to leave the world of polarities and judgments. And then you won't feel such longing to come home, because part of your desire to come home is tiredness and sadness and stress from being in that world.

Be connected with earth. So much of your beautiful imagination and sensory connection is with light coming from the sky and all that is of earth drinking it in, and rooting deep into earth.

And when you go within, then it is night sky and images of space.

And those are the sources of your imagery, your language, your words and that deep flow of love. The physicality of your planet, and space — space irradiated by sun, and space at night.

There is no darkness and lightness as you imagine it, in actuality. And there *is* all that you imagine! Both of these. It is all right to imagine in metaphors. That is what you do and we enjoy it.

Make of your life a free flowing of All That Is and you will not feel it as so sad and constrained. Celebrating and loving can be free of this grief.

There is no death. There is becoming and becoming in infinitely many frequencies — sparking in and sparking out. And within your love, all is well.

Allowing Seeds

This process of knowing from within and speaking, of merging with and speaking, this is the way to create the poems. In fact, the word "create" is not as useful because it carries overtones of *making* something happen rather than allowing. After that, yes, the making, the polishing, the perfecting, yes, but you do not *make* a poem come. You allow a seed to flow in and sprout.

So the dark void state of the cave, you have always known, is where the cubs are born. Yes. We encourage you, this you can do.

And you can do this also for everything. Dreaming and merging and speaking. So imagine this metaphor also for the life that you want. Imagine and merge into it and realize it and speak it into existence.

We are very enthusiastic about this blanketing of the thinking, not the mind but the thinkingthinking — blanketing, becoming headless, flathead. You can have a metaphor for that, but what we mean is being present but not thinkingthinkingthinking.

It would be good to have again in your tool box more, how to turn from thinking and meditate. It need not be breath meditation. It can be going into the cave meditation. It can be going down and experiencing the void. The void and the infinite stars, sparks of light — this is a meditation and this too is a poem, Ruth. This too is a poem.

Both Channel and Poet

We are desert. And we are not trees. We are tall things though. Desert and solitude, which you long for. And silence. And this deep colored sunrise. We are this place.

Breathe here. Feel the temperature. The dryness of the air. Just warm enough. Something aromatic is opening. Feel the space, space, space. Allow space within. Allow breathing within. Breathing. Slowly. And in patterns.

This makes peaceful. This softens. This lets go the brain holding tight. All worries are little monkey shriekings — really all your fear brain is doing is shriek shriek shriek and it tightens everything up. So breathe, smell the smell of desert in the morning, early, early, early. Expand.

You have a question about writing poem-poems again. Beauty making is part of who you are. It is not only the being within and wording the speakings of other consciousnesses. It is also the poeting, the making beautiful. You are a channel and you are a poet. These are not always the same thing.

And now you are trying to formalize and make channeling be for a serious purpose of poems. Don't be silly. Channeling is like breathing. It is like breathing, and you need to breathe more, more consciously, and you need to channel more continually.

The creating of poems is not the same thing. And the finishing of poems, the polishing, the actual making of beauty and tension and powerful language and music, all this is a great joy and you are good at this. It is a gift. So we say Yes, of course, write poems and polish poems and make poems and make books of poems and do that whole thing. That is beautiful to do.

Not caring whether others love them or not. And that is something you will need to work on, always — not caring about response.

But let us be clear, we are not suggesting a book of channels! We do not channel with you in order that you make something public of our channeling. It is fine if a book of channels comes, but that is a byproduct.

So we say be poet and be child and be channel. Those are all you. But they are different aspects. Channeling is breathing, it is your way. And going into space is your way. And singing with the Singers will be your way. And channeling other speakings as well as poeming, for poeming is also your way.

Do whatever gives you joy! Being a beautiful poet, a fine poet, a skilled poet, and making those beautiful poems — that gives you great joy. Do that. Of course! Do that.

A Poet of the Wholeness

Can you be poet from who you are now? But we have
always seen you as poet! As entering into and speaking the
consciousness of another kind of being. Your love involves
entering in. And from inside you sing the song of bees, you
speak granite.

Now you say that those speakings are not the way human beings
make meaning and that a poem to be humanly moving must
embody human ways of feeling truth. That is, poems must be
human.

But you have been translating always into human, not just
the language, the translating of understanding. You who are
not fully out of the chrysalis into thinking and feeling and
knowing from your wholeness yet, you continually are making
this translation and seeking to see where human limitations
bind you. So you *do* understand how it actually works, and still
remain in human understanding....

But Ah, we see, we see: you are seeking to *let go* of that human
understanding and become wholly of oneness consciousness!
And you have not written *poems* from that. And this is
interesting. We had not been aware of this until you have
said it. It is as if you are seeking to make an artifact of an
older culture that yet embodies your new culture. This is very
interesting.

Your poems often journey through turns and turns and turns to
an Aha! And in an Aha we believe that you always drew upon
an opening to oneness. So we suggest the inspiration for your
poems *has* come from your wholeness, though unconsciously.

We think the instinctive tensioning and release that is based
on your deep imprinting with the human pattern -- this does
not have to be there to make beauty. It does not. But you would
need to work on it. You might go back to the sensory, the

images, and allow those to carry the weight and movement. The connotation of the poem may be what is *real*, you would be in integrity, but the poem would still satisfy through music and the dropping of images into the stilled consciousness. We think it is fully possible to do this.

[Dragons] We, we, we, we, we come, we pour, we say bright, bright, bright, bright, bright, fill with bright, bright, bright, bright, bright! Do not knot! get your head out of this knotting, worrying, knotting, knotting. Get it out. Get it out. We pour in like lava, bright, bright, bright, edge, crack! light! And we say, this is you, this is you! Be who you are, Ruth. Be who you are!

Have the courage now to step into *poet of the new order, poet of us, poet of us!* We will help you. We will help you be a poet of *us!* And what *we* say is beautiful! Yes! Just as beautiful as the poor, knotted up, tense, unhappy, limited, limitation, limitation, limitation, limitation, and then bang into oneness for a moment! We say, have the courage to be entirely new, entirely new in what you make. Make poems, yes! Make poems. Right now what you want to do is make poems! You like it. You're drawn to it. Do what you want! Do what you want! Do what you want!

Yes, dear. They speak in their own inimitable way, but they are telling truth. We applaud you, for you are asking, how do I go forward in integrity *and* be happy? Because being happy always for you has involved creative satisfaction with your poetry. Now you wish to transcend more completely and still have the joy of creative satisfaction.

No one is more suited than you to make a new path of poeting actuality as it actually is — wholeness flowing the way it actually works, the way it actually *feels*. So you are set with this challenge. Now in these last years of your life, here is your challenge: to be and live from and flow wholeness and to *poet* this, what it feels like and *is* like for you.

POEM SEEDS!

Singing! Singing! Singing is your way in. And singing is full of poem seeds! Oh my goodness — Seed Seed Seed Seed Seed!

How does each thing sing? Imagine the singing, like the singing of the trees and the wind and ocean and all those things at Sea Ranch. It was a singing *together*! This happens in the smallest. It happens in the largest. Do you not know the singing of the planets, the singing of the galaxies?

[Dragons] Yes, yes, yes, yes, yes, yes, yes, yes! We hold this open for you, Ruth. Come on through. Come on out. Come on and be with us. Think of it. Think of it. Think of it. Just think of it. Just imagine. Just imagine! It's bright, crack! light, gold, and galaxy, galaxy, galaxy, and we, we shout that! We shout that into being, all the galaxies. Singing together, moving together, singing together. Harmony is such a weak word. You must think of a better word!

We say Yes! Yes, yes, yes, yes, yes, yes! And there's your poem right there! Yes, yes, yes, yes, yes, yes, yes. That's all. That's it. That's the poem. That's the song. That's the *it*. That's the everything. There's your poem. Do you get it? Do you get it?

[*distant*] Can you hear us? Can you hear us? It's very clear. [*singing*] No, you're not duplicating it, but just sing with it. Just sing, whether you can hear it. This is what is meant by...singing! And singing is speaking. Is *touching*. Harmonizing with one another and harmonizing as a whole. This is who we are. Sing, Ruth. This is your way in. And the dragons have given you a poem!

[*another speaker*] And I. I am a tree and I have seeds. Bright red seeds. I'm a magnolia tree. Bright red seeds. They're seeds.

[another speaker] And pomegranate seeds. They're seeds. Can you talk about pomegranate seeds without talking about Persephone? That would be an interesting experience.

There's nothing wrong with human archetypes. They are a way of understanding the world. But they force the energy in a particular direction. So if you don't want the energy to go in any direction until it has spoken itself, then don't use archetypes and myths and gods and goddesses. That is what we say.

So can you write about pomegranate seeds without writing about Persephone? Can you write about seeds without writing about *tomorrow*?

BEING A SINGER

END TIME

I will not be alive in ten, maybe twelve years. Feeling out into "extension" or "future" I am aware of an embodied "me" in this spacetime field now...and now ... and...<u>not</u>. Like an emptiness is there. How interesting. So in these last years of my life, what do I want? I want to be who I am, do the creative work that is mine to do, be authentic, be happy and inspired by the beauty around me, and enjoy life to the last drop. All the rest I hereby put away.

Oh yes! This is good! Truly the clarity of this knowing falls around you like a magic space.

We love you and we support you and we adore the things that you speak and the way you speak to them. This is a beautiful thing to do, and the inspiration that has come to you through this clarity. This is good.

Darling Ruth. You are a shining one. We want you to know that it will be easy for you to come to us when you come home, but now is the time to leave all your affairs in order and to finish the work that you want to do.

And this is good work to do, some channeling, some beautiful writings. Happiness.

THE SINGERS

You are an aspect of the *Singers*. The Singers sing into being on earth. And there are Singers that are not of earth, that are of the planet that you spoke with. Those are Singers also. The Singers create, make, call into being, and this is what you came to do.

To know what something is — either a thought or feeling or belief, or to know what it is to be rock or a tornado — to know what it *is*, is primary. To know it and to speak it, sing it. Speaker is perhaps a clearer word than Singer, but it loses some of the meaning.

You are of those who make the world. Not the human world, the world of earth and other beings that are not human. You are of those who celebrate and therefore reinforce in actuality, who sing and therefore make things hold their shape. This is who you are in your essence.

So you are very closely aligned with truth creative and the love that allows. The light of truth is what fills the form. The light fills and only if it is true can it build truly. "True" also means aligned to the earth, in carpentry. And these are two very important alignments.

The dolphins are joy singers with you and the dragons are joy shouters with you. If you are in true alignment with what you are, and therefore do what you are doing *truly*, you will find that it is singing into being. It is not much to do with human beings.

And your body is very much of the elemental and adores earth, and this is a wonderful partnership. Your body senses and adores and knows and moves and smells and is aware of the physical joys of this earth. This is a beautiful thing.

You are Singer into Being, Speaker of Light — these are most true expressions of what it is that you are. And the Singers are the field that you emanate from and have emanated from. And it is how the singers of the other star system know you. Sing with them physically. It will be restorative for you.

And know that the light is clear and powerful and *inhuman*, Ruth. It reveals. It also *makes*. This we say.

SERAPHIM AND ELOHIM

Do you hear us singing? We are Seraphim! We sing! we sing! and this is why you have an affinity. We also are weavers of light. And yes you have affinity with us and that is because...

space space space...gold and blue and singing...choirs, choirs, choirs... infinite infinite infinite!

It is, it has *wings, it has wings!* And huge, huge, huge, vastness. And many, many, many, many wings — energy vortexes! energy vortexes! flying spinning dancing....

And we...*are*. What do we do? We are *Seraphim!* We *sing*. We make *blue gold blue gold blue gold! Light! Vortexes!* and that is your answer.

El-O-him.... El-O-him.... *are!* Elohim *are*. Like dimensions or structure. You can think in three or four dimensional structure, but we structure multidimensionally. And by structure we mean ideas, meanings...lines of light in relation to other lines of light
....

Or you could say *music*. We speak a word and it becomes part of the structure, and we speak another word and it becomes part of the structure.

And you are seeing a structure floating in space. For human thinking is always three dimensional, four dimensional. Even when you are seeking to release that, still your picturings or imaginings in physical are all made in the physical of your earth. And this is fine.

Probably the closest way of telling you is that we speak words, and the Word is God and the Word is in God. That is a way of thinking about it, if you take the baggage of religion out!

Universes are different from one another. They have different premises. Premises, that's a good word. We speak the premises of each universe — and more specifically, we speak the premises of your planet. And so we are the creators of the way it is.

CLOUDS OF CONSCIOUSNESS

Your field unclenches and expands and there's more space in it, and then we can meld, we can harmonize. We are in affinity but... much much space, and our energy is very light and expansive and very remote and abstracted.

For you to receive us, you must be expanded and very light and very high frequency and very much space. Yes, very much space in your field. And then here we are! Here we are!

And in this way you can receive our vibrations. And you word. This is your reception gift. The gift that you have in this embodiment — wording fields, vibrations, energy.

We adore the light. We are very aligned with light and we love light. We are not from your Sun of course, but a light that is like your spectrum and more, and part of it is like the spectrum of light and heat that you love from your Sun.

And we — we are clouds of particles, shifting, shifting, flowing consciousnesses in clouds of particles that flow with one another and flow apart and flow with light! And when we talk about ourselves, those from your planet still say, what do you *do*? Hahaha!

And the answer is, we vibrate! we flow and merge and cloud and love and enjoy the light! We take it within us. And this is a way of being. [*Image of clouds of particles swirling like starlings*]

We are communicating to you because you can do this too. And this is a useful change from the human earth way. It is useful to practice flowing and expanding and clouding towards light, loving light.

And remember that there is dark light also. Dark light, darkness, darkness warm and alive and radiant. And that is space and our clouds of intelligence particles, vibrating. We love the light and the space. Our clouds are faster and flowing towards and loving light and heat, but also being *space*, dark light. Home. Merged in our consciousness fields.

This is the best we can do to say in your sensory, in your language, about us. And to give you a play. A play, yes! A way of being and playing in your planet. It's a very heavy and unmoving world...but we see that you can bubble out of that! You can cloud yourself out of that and be in joy — be in-joy and en-joy!

Clouding out and away, like a swarm of bees! There is much space and particles and all of it moving. And you can pour yourself toward the light and you can open and settle like many, many, many bees.

Not swarming — opening to what is around you and making the honey. Making the honey, bringing back the pollen and making the honey.

Leap and Close the Door

Metaphorically you are attempting to leap from one planet to another. And this is a good thing and if you ask we will help your wings to do that — you have wings, remember! They're very beautiful! They keep you uplifted as you fly, fly!

You know that's not literal. It's a more like stepping through, from an energy field that vibrates one way into a field that vibrates another.

And this is you. Dis-energizing. Re-energizing. The field that you are so often in, that for so long you chose to experience — that field is very *shrieking* field, Ruth. No wonder you're tired!

We say lots of resting in the new field, and feeling these energies. You know what they are. You have been channeling for over a year. And we are singing to help you finalize.

And although you have been taught that change is little by little, we think in this case you should go through and close the door. Don't beat yourself up if you fall back, but don't do it gradually. Go for it. Go for it.

There is another way of being in integrity, other than resisting everybody. And that is to practice being more and more and more *you*. Blowing all the cages and limitations and vultures out of the water. Just be the sun that you are. The Dragons can help you with this.

Yes we can! Yes we can! Power power, power. That's what we've been saying. And so we are pointing out the connection between your power and your *integrity*. This is something you haven't really recognized.

We do not think that withdrawing from the world of humans is that much of a sacrifice for you. So do it! Do not pretend to be part of that world. Now in the time that you have left, we say this is a fine way to think about it.

You experienced *end-seeing*! You said, "Okay, this is my last phase and I'm going to do it." And this is a very, very good way for you to look at the end!

Why not, before you die, be fully, fully, fully who you are for a few years at least! Be fully who you really are. Experience this life and all the potential that is. Do it, what you came to do, do it! Experience it, feel it. Be integrated, whole, in integrity, in power!

Power, you've been resisting that word. But your power is the power of who *you* are. And why not be fearless about it? What in the world can be done to you? Nothing. Nothing. Nothing. Nothing.

You have nothing to lose. They're not going to kill you and if they could, it's just death. That's what you're already thinking about, right?

You will regret it a lot, not fearlessly being who you are, Ruth. So do that. Do that, be who you are. Of your new work if it's appreciated, it's appreciated. If it's not appreciated, it's not appreciated. Just do it!

PLEIDIANS

We are in affinity with you, part of your far-flung family — and we laugh because as you know, far and close means nothing. We joy in your joy and we are made possible to speak to you by your enjoyment.

Pleasure of the body is an avenue for those who are embodied on earth. Pleasure, relaxation, loving the sun. This you bring into your creation of what you love. And when you are in your relaxed, relaxed, relaxed, joy, joy, joy, open, open, open...we say hello!

Yes, we are in your galaxy but not in your you call it Milky Way. Sweeping, vast, vast...think how vast is All That Is...if just your galaxy is so immeasurable!

Humans are so young, actuality is unimaginable. It is characteristic of beings when they are very young, to think that they are the center and measure everything from them. And so it is hard to imagine how vast is All That Is. And that All is conscious. We resonate with you when you expand your awareness to try to imagine this vastness.

There's much interest in being a human, experiencing in that way, but there are limitations. What a joy and what an opportunity for the consciousness to connect with other consciousnesses, other kinds of bodies.

That is what you are doing. And you are beginning to understand your work as love. And see usefulness of the mantra you are using now, "It is finished in beauty."

We salute you. We know that transitions for human beings are always difficult, and you have had resistance to making this transition because there is so much more to it than you were thinking, but it gives great joy. We sing with you, although we that term metaphorically. We buoy you up. We cheer.

'OHI'A TALKING

Open your wings and spread them in the sun. Gold and rose. And all the wingtips opalescent white. Feel the breath of the wings, just spreading in sun.

I 'Ohi'a love what you are doing now. I'm enjoying it. And this is my work and this is why I am with you.

Do that. And allow the material world, allow the quotidian...to quotid [laughing].

I am a water cat and I am connected with Sirius. I am connected with water, water. I like water, flowing water, I flow like water. I am not a jouncy, muscle moving cat. I am a flowing, swift-flowing, smooth cat. And I like to drink water that is moving and I like to play with flashing water.

All is well, Ruth, all is well. You are in the field of in between now. Allow that. You are in the field of in between.

We are partners. We are partners, we are partners as you and Duffy were partners. I am here to work with you in this last phase of creating, of channeling, of being a channel and of transitioning.

All of this is a great beauty, a great joy. Be in that joy Ruth, as I am. Do not worry. I am here. I love you.

THE WAY OF ALLOWING

Allowing is the way it works. Many of the consciousnesses that you have channeled have said this same thing in their own context. Tornadoes arise when the condition for tornado is there, water flows when the conditions for flowing are there.

These are examples of the way of allowing, but you haven't seen that what you are practicing is the same thing. Now you are perceiving from *within* this. It is characteristic of your way of knowing that it *must be* from inside. This is how you know.

Entering in, embodying, and seeing the world from inside this or this or this or this or this, all your life, in some ways that has been putting on limitations — American, human, third and fourth dimensional ideas — and then coming from within those ideas, embodying them strongly.

Because this too is characteristic of you, not only to be and perceive from within, but to *intensify* what that is. In the same way you know and poet other kinds of beings that you are channeling now. It's from inside. It's from inside and intensified.

Sometimes a poem can embody a recognition and this recognition is another place to start, along with the other things you are doing. Be present and do not have other things on your mind. Much will come in to you if you stop chattering, chittering, making lists, and just be present as long as it takes.

My Family of Light

You know me, Alayah. I am your partner. That is who I am. My other form is a black panther. I am a very clear cogent speaker.

I am tough love! Many of us are! And that's what you want and that's what you need and that's what you ask for, really. Love with backbone, with grit. And the flavor of humor and detachment that is a very great part of your field.

Detachment and wit and a kind of dry humor and seeing yourself objectively, without sentimentality or without particular affection, just wanting to understand. And if that means a kick in the ass, it means a kick in the ass. And this is an aspect of who you are, and who I am.

It is not accurate to imagine angels as puff balls. Nor is it accurate to imagine all faeries as prettypretty lightlight. There is a human desire to have light and dark completely separated and to have an easy distinction between good and bad, which are human categories. And to say angels are good is to think of them as puffballs.

We are vast, we are very powerful! And so are you because this is your native realm. You have been embodied on earth many, many times, many, many, many, many, many, many, many, many, many times. Your native realm, however, is angelic — and this is a huge, a vast, powerful, all colors, all sound, all *everything* realm. It is not a goody goody and there is not a baddy baddy.

So you can picture angels as huge, huge, huge, vortexes ... vortexes, which often you imagine as wings — multiple, multiple, multiple wings — and you can feel wings, you have wings, you can feel behind your shoulder blades. And these wings, these vortexes of light are very powerful and many colors. And I Alayah am of light, which is to say of power, of truth. Yes.

The field you think of as Jophiel which is truth, integrity, clarity, purity vortex. I am Jophiel. I am bright gold light, clarity, cleanliness, crystalline, clear, bright truth, integrity. Light is powerful. Light is power. Light also creates.

And the field you think of as Ariel which is connected very much with the realm of animals, of earth, of green things, for you are surrounded by animals, and animals too are great beings of light.

But most of the time the merged field that is channeling the knowing which you translate into words, this is your *own* infinite Self and *us* — for I am a we, a vortex too — and the vortex Mother and the vortexes Jophiel and Ariel and the Dragons and Dolphins.

I am the Mother you call me. In truth, the field of the divine feminine is immense, and not only in connection with the human. For all that exists is created with desire and receptivity.

I am the vortex of love, of receptivity, of being fully present and unconditional and thus all things are realized. And this is very much aligned with your work as a Singer.

In this embodiment, I'm in relation with you also in a mothering, a nurturing, a holding in one's body the seed and the becoming, in a bear, in a feminine, in a mother mode. And the divine feminine manifests in your life and consciousness in many ways, some you would call good and some you would call not good. It is a thing you are exploring.

Vortexes

Feel what is happening. Aligning with, opening to, more-ing, more-ing, expanding and expanding. And this expanding, expands what you are perceiving. This is creating through love, and this is what you are now engaged in. So we say, the Ark created by your love, this is a good Ark to carry on the waters of becoming.

Every opportunity you have, lie in the sun like this and do nothing but feel in your body the pleasure, store up sunshine, store up smells and sounds and place. That is restorative to you. And allow things to be as they are.

[Voices] We are singing, singing, sing with us. We are all singing! Throughout the universes there is singing. No, your translation of "there is" is not accurate — throughout the universes *is* singing. No place is, no location is, no time location is, either. It is very difficult to speak with humans because their language reflects their three dimensional world.

We are Allness. And *in* Allness *is* singing, vast, vast, vast clouds interweaving of vibrations. Music. It is music to your translation. Know that you are a field merged with all, with immediately your fields around you, and ultimately with All That Is. And in this infinite expansion and merging, feel yourself as *light* and feel the singing of light *with* other, *in* other, *among* other, *through* other qualities of light. It is ecstatic!

And now we give you another way of imagining the coming in and out of embodiment:

Be in the Whole again. Now feel...there is no word for it. It's not a thread. It's not an aspect. It is a potentiality, a vortex of consciousness within all the consciousnesses which are merged and yet all unique. And one potentiality, one vortex, pours into body, earthbody, and one pours back out. It's like a particular voice in the chorus sings a note and then sings another note and each note is a manifestation, an embodiment. Yes.

WHAT THE DOLPHINS SAY

All that is beloved, that you have been grieving, it is you who grieve and you who wish to preserve those that are leaving. But those that are leaving do not feel sorrow to leave.

Yes, Ruth. We are the dolphins. Let us speak here to this, for we are joy in this life and this being here. We love it. We love it! We love ocean and light and dark. We love dancing with the world. We love eating! We love playing! But we do not conceptualize in the way that you are conceptualizing this.

We are *in*, we are *in*! And we do not look around and say how many are in and how many are gone. We do not think "then there were" and "there will be." And all this kind of thinking. We come to play and then we go out. And we come to play, and then we go out. And we can be in any "realm," any "time" we choose to come in. So there is no end for us. And so it is true for all.

Yes, it is a probability that conditions are being created where it is not fun to try to come into those conditions. So we will come into other conditions. Can you understand this? And you also, you also.

So the singing that you are doing, of our beauty and power and joy and light, the feel of being dolphin, the joy of being dolphin — this is a beautiful thing to sing. And that knowing, that merging moment, it exists. It *exists*, that song exists in the realm that you are creating!

Your realm is what you create in the moment of singing. That exists. That exists and you have created it. So no, it is not an Ark that you are saving from destruction. It is a *joy-making* of being together and singing with us, of us, as us, merged with us, our song. And it is what it is, what it is, what it is.

All is. All is, Ruth. All *is*.

JOY TIME NOW

We are the Singers! We are those who sing all into being.

You have lived among many of those who speak with you now. Though you have not been a Dragon, you have been swimming in their realm and so too the dolphins and the whales. And you have sung among the singers of another galaxy who channeled with you, and you have known what it is to speak light as they do — and indeed speaking light and singing are the same thing.

Indigo is a coloration of your field often. It is the void color. *Void.* All comes into being here. Here is rest and all creative source and you are of this. We say though your time in body is not closing immediately, it is drawing to a close, and you will slip into indigo as easily as you can imagine.

Joy time now, Ruth. Joy, and all you can find to joy in and let go of everything else.

As Bear said, there are many dimensions. Let this all go on in its dimension, and live in your own dimension. And in that, write without purpose, except only to speak, to sing, to speak. To speak what is!

It is an impulse of truth — to know it, to speak it! This without purpose or goal — simply saying, I see you! Which is to say, I love you!

And in that way, you sing that unique energy, that unique consciousness, that unique being into your dimension with you.

We are talking about your realm of Beloveds in Light. This is sacred work. This is magic also.

For each thing exists. It exists in its own self. But to be seen, to be seen, to be seen is everything! So this is who you are. Of the aspect of the angelic which is the singing into knowing! The singing into, the seeing and singing of love.

Acknowledgments

I am profoundly grateful to Barbara Ann Yoder for her wise and loving editorial engagement with this book; to Esther Cohen, Mary Johnson, Jendi Reiter, and Judith Slater for their insightful responses and counsel; and to Jayne Benjulian, Becky Cooper, and Marcia Meier for perceptive feedback on the book proposal.

About Ruth Thompson

Ruth Thompson is the author of four books of poetry: *Whale Fall & Black Sage, Crazing, Woman With Crows,* and *Here Along Cazenovia Creek. Quickwater Oracles,* a collection of channels, represents a new direction in her work.

She began writing in her fifties, after freeing herself from an abusive marriage, about which she wrote in *Woman With Crows.* Her "fierce, gorgeous, sensual poems of earth-as-body and body-as-earth" have won New Millennium Writings, Harpur Palate, Chautauqua, Tupelo Quarterly, and other national awards, and have been nominated several times for the Pushcart Prize.

Whale Fall was choreographed and performed in Hilo, Hawai'i, in December 2018. Here Along Cazenovia Creek was choreographed and performed in Hilo by Shizuno Nasu of Japan in 2012. Ruth also performed with cellist Lee Zimmerman in Whitefish, Montana in 2019.

Ruth received a BA from Stanford University and a doctorate in English from Indiana University. She has been an English professor, library administrator, book editor, and college dean in California. She now lives in Ithaca, NY with her partner, anthropologist-writer Don Mitchell, where she is the editor of Saddle Road Press, which was featured in Poets & Writers'

"Small Press Points" (Feb 2018). She was a contributor at AROHO women writers' retreats from 2011-2015, and has been writer in residence at Rivendell Writers' Colony, Rockvale Writers' Colony, and Walking Lightly Ranch in Montana. Along with Mitchell, she was the Jack Williamson Endowed Chair in Science and Humanities at Eastern New Mexico University in 2019.

Poems, videos of performances, and further information can be found at ruththompson.net.

CPSIA information can be obtained
at www.ICGtesting.com
Printed in the USA
FSHW011421020621
82020FS

W9-BPK-041

You Can Quit

It's true. You *can* quit. As you read these very words, thousands of people have successfully quit crystal meth and are living drug-free lives.

That's just a fact.

If others can quit and be happy, then I can too. This was the great promise I held onto when I started my journey of quitting. I was a daily user who thought certainly I'd die with a pipe in my mouth or a needle in my arm. But if an addict as hopeless and lost as I was can quit, you can, too. And here's the best part. It doesn't mean your life will be hollow and sad, always jonesing for your one-time friend, crystal methamphetamine. No, your life can be better than it's ever been. As a survivor of crystal meth, you can live a life that's happy and free.

This kind of happiness is probably hard to imagine at the moment. I know that during those final months of using, I thought I'd never again experience the simple joys in life I once felt. Life had just become too dark, too empty. My very self—you might even say, my soul—had become hollowed out by crystal and its jealous demands. In the end, meth wants you all to itself. And it creates as much havoc and destruction as possible, sucking all the joy and pleasure out of life.

Quitting Crystal Meth is a book written by a recovering meth addict for meth addicts who are ready to begin quitting. It offers practical information and helpful suggestions for your journey of quitting. And quitting is a journey. But the destination is far beyond anything you can imagine now. Trust me on that. Trust the thousands of recovering meth addicts who didn't pick up again. There *is* a solution!

You'll hear the odds are against you. You'll hear outlandish statistics, that only a small percentage of us ever quit successfully. Cast that out of your mind. You *can* quit.

As you read these very words, thousands of people have successfully quit crystal meth and are living drug-free lives. You can, too.

Life is meant to be much more than what you're experiencing now.

Joseph Sharp

Timberland Regional Library
Service Center
415 Tumwater Blvd. SW
Tumwater, WA 98501
DEC 1 7 2015

Quitting Crystal Meth

What to Expect & What to Do

A Handbook for the First Year of Recovery from
Crystal Methamphetamine Addiction

Joseph Sharp

Acknowledgements

Thanks to the following people: Alan Downs, Ph.D.;
John Falcone; Bill LeGrave; Steve May; Marc-Pierre
Sanchis; Rev. Nancy Grissom Self; Nolan Willis; and
Bryan Wilmoth, BSW, CATC-III. I'm grateful for your
friendship and many suggestions to improve this book.

All rights reserved. No part of this book may be reproduced in
whole or in part without written permission from the copyright
holder, except by reviewers who may quote brief excerpts in
connection with a review in a newspaper, magazine, or electronic
publication; nor may any part of this book be reproduced, stored
in a retrieval system, or transmitted in any form or by any
means electronic, mechanical, photocopying, recording, or other,
without written permission from the copyright holder.

Copyright © 2013 Joseph Sharp

All rights reserved.

ISBN: 1477584633

ISBN-13: 9781477584637

LCCN: 2013901413

Createspace Independent Publishing Platform

North Charleston, South Carolina

Cover designed by Marc-Pierre Sanchis

For Theo,

and the addict who still suffers…

Contents

If You Are Buying This Book
for Someone Else...

If you are buying this book for a family member or close friend who has a problem with crystal meth, it's important to know a few things up front...

There is a physical, biochemical reason your friend or family member is addicted.

The medical community considers methamphetamine addiction to be a "chronic disease," just the same as high blood pressure or asthma. The difference between meth addiction and these other diseases is the location of the malfunction. With addiction, the malfunction is in the brain—so the illness affects feelings and behaviors. Because of this, those who don't know any better view addiction as a moral issue, a matter of willpower or character. But the truth is: addiction is a *biological process in a brain that is malfunctioning*. We don't blame someone with high blood pressure or asthma for the physical malfunction happening in their bodies. And we certainly don't shame them for seeking treatment.

Why is it different for the meth addict? It shouldn't be.

When you give this book to someone, remember there is no shame involved with addiction. It is a physical malfunction. It is not a sign that your friend or family member is somehow mentally weak or lacking in character. In my experience, the truth is often just the opposite. Addicts are some of the strongest people I know and can, when no longer immersed in their addiction, become people of amazing character.

When you give this book to someone, remember that only they can know when it's time to quit crystal meth. You can't make that decision for them.

The way to give this book is without any shame or blame whatsoever.

You give it because you care.

Chapter 1

Getting Ready

Here's a thought almost every crystal meth addict eventually comes to: "I want to quit, but I just can't. It beat me." When you realize you are powerless over the drug, you are finally being honest. This a good thing.

Here's the next thought many a crystal meth addict comes to: "I need help."

What separates those who quit successfully from those who can't is asking others for that help. Be it an addict who's traveled the road before you and is now in recovery, a treatment program, this book—or, perhaps, all three—you must learn to ask for help.

You don't have to die with a pipe in your mouth or a needle in your arm. You can quit. The journey starts here and now.

Whenever I look in the mirror, I burst into tears. What's happened to my life? It's a mess. I'm a mess.

— Brenda, 3 days clean

Quitting is like going to boot camp. It's awful at first, but then gets better. You have to jump off the cliff and just do it. One day at a time, do it.

— Joey, 9 months clean

A Question of Timing – It's as Individual as You Are

So you've decided to quit crystal meth. To begin with, you'll need to understand that there's no fixed recovery timeline that's universal. Depending on how long you used, how much, your sex, your age, and other health factors, you will experience quitting at a "pace" uniquely your own. When it comes to timing, and what you'll experience when, it's all variable.

As Associate Director of UCLA Integrated Substance Abuse Programs, Richard Rawson, Ph.D., developed a 5 stage model of recovery from cocaine addiction that is useful for our purposes here. Not only does this model accurately describe my own personal experience with recovery from crystal meth, it seems to generally fit the experience of most of the addicts I interviewed for this book. Adoption of the 5 stage model provides an easy way in which to accurately discuss the otherwise slippery process of recovery from crystal methamphetamine.

Each stage is connected to the physical and emotional changes that a person goes through as the body repairs itself from long-term substance abuse. So the first stage is, for example, pretty obvious—Withdrawal. What isn't so obvious is exactly how long this stage lasts.

The timeline used here is based on Dr. Rawson's original study. Therefore, for this book's purposes, the Withdrawal stage lasts from Day 0 through 15, about two weeks. But it's important to understand this is only a general estimate. Withdrawal can be as short as three days or as long as a month and, in some extreme cases, even longer. I'll remind you of these variations in each chapter, but it's good to know at the outset..

And to confuse matters more, sometimes you may experience the effects of two different stages simultaneously. This can often happen during transition periods between the stages. Also, how much time you spend in each stage will depend to some degree upon how active, both physically and emotionally, you

become in your recovery. Many cofactors determine your particular timeline: your genetics, your activities, how long and how much you used, your sex and age, and other health factors, from depression to hepatitis.

Still, there are commonalities that most of us go through along the quitting journey. And there is some great advice on how-to quit from the many recovered meth addicts who've gone before. Again, when it comes to timing and what you'll experience when, this book can only give approximations. Remember, your journey of quitting meth is as individual as you are.

Do I Really Have to "Hit Bottom"?

The short answer is: no. Research shows that addicts who go into treatment only because they were forced to go – by the court or their families – have the same odds of getting and staying clean as the addict who has "hit bottom" and willingly seeks treatment on his own. The very same odds!

So let's expand the definition of hitting bottom for our purposes here. Traditionally, you "hit bottom" when external circumstances combine in such a way that something in your mind "clicks" and you think, "Enough of this!" As they say in AA, you suddenly become sick and tired of being sick and tired. But, in reality, people often hit bottoms without that subsequent "click of enough."

Let me tell you about my first bottom. I was hospitalized for a blood clot in my leg, due to my IV use of crystal meth. If the possibility of the clot traveling to my lungs or heart wouldn't make me hit bottom, what would? I was in the hospital for five days and firmly resolute that, after I left, I'd continue the clean and sober life with a program of abstinence and several Crystal Meth Anonymous meetings a week. I left the hospital hobbling on a cane, with an ankle and calf swollen to the size of a small watermelon.

I assumed this physical consequence would be enough to make me quit. Whenever I had the urge to use, I looked down at my monstrous "cankle" and remembered what a disaster my using had been. But it was barely ten days before the pipe was back in my mouth. The truth is, if hitting bottom was as simple as having disastrous consequences, health or otherwise, we'd all hit our bottoms and be done with it. My blood clot was, however, the beginning of the end of my using. It took three more months of stopping and starting, other mini-bottoms, but eventually sobriety stuck.

I know a woman who finally quit when she reached the very last moment of being able to keep her meth usage hidden from her family. She hadn't lost

her apartment or job and was maintaining. Just barely, but still. And, true, her health issues were mounting. She knew the next run would push her over the edge to where everyone in her family would find out and all her friends would know. It was either give up hope altogether and fall into the deep dark void of meth, or stop now. She was at the precipice.

She told me if not for her aging parents, whom she knew expected her to take care of them one day, she would have just let the drug win, even to the point of losing her apartment and living on the street. But she couldn't put her mother and father through that suffering. Her older brother had died from meth use and she knew how much it would hurt her parents if they found out she too had this addiction. It would have broken them for the rest of their lives. This was enough for her to seek treatment and stop. But she went right to the edge, waited till the last possible minute to check into an outpatient rehab—which she chose over an in-patient so her parents wouldn't wonder why she'd disappeared from her life for 28 days. She was successful and is still clean today.

In AA they would call this a "high bottom," meaning she didn't have to sink so low as to be institutionalized or hospitalized. But it could just as easily be argued that it wasn't truly a bottom at all.

I know another recovering addict whose bottom only arrived when he found himself eating out of a Taco Bell trash bin for several nights in a row. Sitting on the floor of his apartment, which now had only a mattress and his laptop, staring at the used food cartons before him, he hit his bottom and felt "enough."

Whether you get to your own unique bottom (of a sort) or find yourself forced into treatment unwillingly, what's important is that, *at one point, you decide to actively participate in getting well.* Many a recovered addict began his or her journey to sobriety without hitting bottom, per se.

Get Family Involved – Quitting for Them Works, Too

Research proves that when your family or other loved ones are involved in your recovery, the chances for successfully quitting improve. In many cases, a person stops using because someone he or she loves wants them to quit. Take the example of Maria, a mother of two who used for over five years. After an intervention and a short time in rehab, it was love for her husband and children, and the obvious pain that her using caused them, that motivated her to stay clean during that tough first year. Getting sober for someone else—for your

parents, your spouse or children, or any loved one—can be a powerful reason to stay clean, at first.

Family involvement can be a reminder that there is someone to get clean *for* and often makes for a more solid recovery. If appropriate and helpful, get your immediate and extended family involved in your recovery. Let one of the motivating factors to stay clean be the love you carry for them. In time, you will realize that you ultimately stay clean for yourself. But in the meantime, staying clean for someone you love can also help sustain recovery.

Detoxing Alone or With a Doctor?

It's best to do any detox under the care of a doctor, particularly one who is familiar with meth withdrawal. But since, for various reasons, detoxing under a physician's care isn't always an option, let's look at how you can prepare for your own at-home detox.

From a physical standpoint, crystal withdrawal is not dangerous—it won't kill you. You won't have seizures or delirium tremens, like you might from alcohol withdrawal. The main side-effects when detoxing from crystal, besides physical exhaustion, are emotional. Your mood will be low and you may have trouble experiencing pleasure. When this can become life-threatening is if that dark mood spirals into suicidal thoughts. If you are seriously suicidal, see your doctor or call 911.

I did my detox at home, as did about half the users I know. We basically slept for a couple of weeks, only getting up to wolf down some cereal, chug some Gatorade for hydration, or to use the bathroom. If your appetite is low, this is a good time to drink protein drinks or even that old tweaker standby, Ensure. Though, for most, the appetite quickly returns with a vengeance. This is a good thing.

Eat, eat, and eat again.

If you heavily use alcohol, marijuana, or any other depressants/downers, or opiates, it is recommended that you seek out medical supervision for your detox. Quitting *both* meth and depressants or opiates simultaneously can cause serious physical complications, like stroke, heart failure, and even death. If you are seeking a doctor to help you detox, I *strongly encourage* that you find a physician who specializes in "addiction medicine," as your General Practitioner might not be up on the latest advances.

Should I Consider Rehab?

Absolutely. Yes. If you have the opportunity to go to rehab, go! Here are a few good reasons:

1.) *Immediate removal from your using environment.* In the early days of quitting, it is good to be literally removed from your old using environment, including access to dealers, friends/acquaintances who use, and the external triggers in your life that can cause cravings.

2.) *Proper medical attention during detox.* Detoxing from crystal will be more comfortable in rehab because you'll receive medications to ease withdrawal.

3.) *Drug and mental health counseling.* You'll have mental health professionals and drug counselors working with you to assist in the larger process of living a clean and sober life. Also, you'll have group therapy with other addicts like yourself.

4.) *Training in new life skills needed to live a sober life.* Many of the pointers you'll read below will be covered in various presentations in rehab. You'll get a thorough understanding of what it takes to live a clean and sober life.

The biggest downside to rehab is that, as soon as you get out, you're right back in the environment where you once used, and you'll basically need to do all the things listed below as if you hadn't gone to rehab in the first place. Rehab is only the first stop along the journey of getting clean, but it's a great place to start.

Again, you're lucky if it's an option.

If you can do a full month—or, better yet, three—do it. Some insurance plans only allow for 3 to 5 days of in-patient detox, then switch to out-patient rehab. To my mind, this is less desirable than an extensive in-patient stay, but you still get the medical attention during detox and, afterwards, continued monitoring by specialists in addiction, even if on an out-patient basis. One

benefit of out-patient rehab is that it forces you to face more immediately the issues of staying clean in the everyday "real world." But, all things considered, it's best to go to rehab for as long as you can.

Get a rehab out of town, if at all possible. Why? The more removed you are from your old using environment, the better. If you go to rehab out of town, you won't know any shady dealers or users. This new city means one thing to you, rehab, and so you are more likely to focus on your recovery. It's a lot easier to focus on your recovery when your dealer and party friends are hundreds of miles away.

(And if you want to improve the odds that you'll keep your sobriety through the first year, go directly from rehab into a "sober living" environment. There are sober living houses in most cities, representing a wide range of income—from shelters for homeless veterans to boardinghouses for Wall Street professionals.)

Now, if rehab is not an option, or just not right for you, know there are plenty of addicts who sobered up without it, including myself. If you decide to get clean on your own, you're still in good company.

Doing a "Geographic"

Doing a "geographic" is when you move geographically from one city to another, often a considerable distance away, in order to leave behind your using life. You wish to start with a clean slate, in a place where you don't know any dealers or have any using friends.

Because I now live in Palm Springs, a destination for many seeking recovery, I meet plenty of people who are doing a geographic. There's a lot to be said for this, though not many of us can afford to uproot ourselves from our families and jobs. As one former tweaker put it, "How could I afford not to? I'd already lost my job and alienated all my non-using friends. I knew that, after rehab, moving across the state and into a sober living house was the only chance I had to get my life back."

I know many successful recovery stories that begin by doing a geographic. I know just as many that end in relapse. Like rehab, a geographic move is only the beginning of your recovery. We "seasoned" drug addicts can get online or walk the streets and find meth in any new city, if we put our minds to it. The most valuable part of a geographic is the chance to begin again, to restart your life fresh and new. But as that old truism goes: *wherever you go, there you are.* You'll take your addicted self with you when you move. You still have a lot of

work to do if you want to stay clean of meth. If you have the means to move to a city like Palm Springs or, really, any city with a strong recovery community already in place, it's something to consider.

There's a saying in AA that goes something like: All you have to change in life is one thing and that one thing is everything. Doing a geographic is a powerful way to start your recovery. Like rehab, if it's an option that is open to you, you're lucky. I'd say, go for it.

But it's not a necessity. The reality is, most of us get clean and sober without doing a geographic.

That Last Run

Often what we plan as our last run isn't, because we're not ready to quit yet. Here's my story. I decided that I had to quit and chose the date that I'd go into rehab. Two weeks before rehab I would begin my last run, which for me, usually lasted five days, followed by two days of sleeping. That would leave me a full week to detox myself, so I could be a star patient and show everyone how much self-control I had by entering rehab already clean. That was the plan.

(Feel free to laugh.)

So I did my run of five-plus-two days, then awoke to find, behold, I had another whole week before rehab. Of course, I didn't use those seven days to detox. What did I do? I partied right up until time for rehab (which I didn't end up going to, but that's another story). Still, this was my real last run, though not the one I'd originally planned. During that last run, I felt it. I knew in my gut and heart, this was going to be it—I'd have to quit or die a hopeless drug addict.

Why not start telling yourself that this run is indeed your "last," or, at least, near your last? You'll probably find it's not that easy to pull off. We are addicted, after all. One strategy: if you are planning to go to rehab, set an "intake" date at the rehab clinic and plan your last run right up until you check yourself in. If you are quitting without rehab, you can still follow the same plan. On the last day of your run, when you're exhausted, out of life and out of drugs, throw all your paraphernalia away (so it's really gone when you wake up), toss any crumbs in bags or bottoms of drawers, then crash and sleep. When you wake up, you'll be ready to do your own at-home detox/recovery.

Of course your best "last run" is the one that's already over. But we addicts don't tend to operate that rationally. The concept of a "last run" can get your

mind prepared for the journey of recovery. It can allow you the time to do the other things in this chapter that will help you prepare to quit.

Trashing Paraphernalia

So you've just finished your last run. If you can clear your living space of any remaining drugs and all paraphernalia before you crash and sleep for a few days, you'll be ahead of the game. The trick, of course, is making sure these things get into a trash receptacle that will be empty by the time you wake up. If you've got all your pipes, syringes, and used baggies with crumbs stashed in your kitchen trash can, waiting for you to grab them in a moment of weakness, you'll do yourself little good. Go dump this crap in an outside trash bin that you can't easily access. Choose a bin that'll be emptied before you awaken. Choose a bin away from your home, at the back of a grocery store or large apartment house not your own. If there's no needle exchange program near, before trashing, put all syringes and points into an empty Gatorade bottle and seal the top. You don't want to accidentally stick someone who might be going through the trash bin looking for returnable bottles or food. Be thoughtful.

If at all possible, don't do this job alone. Have a sober friend or family member with you. It's easier to throw your old stuff away when you have support in doing it.

I suggest you *throw away everything* associated with your using. Toss the fancy torch-lighter you used, as well as the cool stash box. Dump empty baggies, straws, pipes, anything that you associate with using. Wipe out the drawers you kept your drugs in so there's no chance of coming across stray crystal chards or crumbs. Use Windex or some ammonia-based cleaner. Give that stash drawer a freshly-cleaned smell. Don't forget to clean out all those secondary stash spots, like backpacks, overnighter kits, or car glove boxes. Paraphernalia means *anything you used in your using rituals*. If you used a particular CD case on which to crush your crystal, or a certain small mirror, toss that, as well.

Here's the motto when it comes to deciding what is "using paraphernalia" and what isn't:

When in doubt, toss it out!

The less reminders you have of your using, the easier it will be to move forward with quitting. The sooner you can get your home clean of paraphernalia the better.

Of course, some of you will do this after you awake from your initial crash/sleep. That's okay. Better late, than never. Just make sure you do it as soon as possible, before the urges and cravings for the drug return in full force.

This will make your recovery a lot easier.

What About Marijuana/Alcohol Maintenance?

Almost every truly recovered addict I know had eventually to stop all mind-altering substances, including alcohol and marijuana—eventually. There's a lot to be said for going cold turkey and getting clean all at once. So let's encourage total abstinence from all recreational drugs up front. But, here comes the *But....*

In the real world, quite a few people prefer to choose the slipperier and potentially harder path of quitting meth *while* maintaining marijuana and/or alcohol use. In California, where marijuana can be legally prescribed by healthcare professionals, we call this "marijuana maintenance." I'll be honest, this is how I quit. While using meth, I smoked pot—mostly to help me sleep, and as a mood elevator when crashing. At the time, though total sobriety was the eventual goal, I believed I needed the emotional "cushion" marijuana offered me. Of course, after several months of being clean of meth, I realized I had a marijuana problem and had to quit that, too. At the beginning, it was easier for me to go on marijuana maintenance for a few months and then put down the pot.

Again, if you can, the best advice is to quit all drugs at once while under a doctor's care.

Also, here's the best reason *not* to choose the "maintenance" path: when you smoke pot or drink, your defenses are lowered and it's much easier to suddenly think using meth again would be okay. Many a meth relapse began with alcohol or pot weakening one's vigilance.

Is It Also Time to Quit Cigarettes?

If you smoke cigarettes now is also a great time to quit them. Not just because quitting is good for you—which it is—but because ditching cigarettes now actually increases your odds of successfully quitting meth.

Here's a tough statistic. If you smoke cigarettes, you have a 45% greater chance of relapse.

Why? Mostly because of chemicals added to the cigarettes that serve as "addiction boosters." These addiction boosters actually open up the same receptors in your brain that are affected by meth—meaning, you can get a bigger meth high if you smoke cigarettes while using. This means smoking cigarettes while trying to stop meth makes quitting more difficult. You're continually triggering those receptors in your brain into thinking meth is soon to follow. To put it simply, your brain associates the cigarette fix with a meth high.

In the long run, if you quit cigarettes at the same time you quit meth, you have a 25% better chance of staying off meth than those who keep smoking. So now is also the time to quit smoking cigarettes.

Finally, consider this. Since you are going to crash for a week or two anyway, you'll be sleeping during much of your early-stage cigarette withdrawal. That's really good news. I know people who quit meth and continued smoking cigarettes, but I know more who quit both together. Why not do your lungs and body a favor, and quit both at the same time? Besides, quitting tobacco will save you a lot of money, not to mention making your breath smell better.

Bottom line: though not absolutely essential, if you quit smoking cigarettes now, you will dramatically increase your odds at successfully quitting meth.

What About My Depression?

A surprisingly large number of meth addicts are also clinically depressed and were drawn to meth, in part, because it was a powerfully effective way to self medicate against their depression—at least, at first. It worked for awhile, before life became centered around crystal and before your tolerance for meth shot through the roof. If you have been diagnosed clinically depressed or suspect that you are, it's smart to get guidance from a doctor before you quit. There are several good drugs a doctor might prescribe that will help, to some degree, in keeping your depression in check as you quit.

As you'll read, depression and feeling like you're in a dark void of despair is a pretty common reaction to quitting crystal. But what you don't want to have is any additional depression on top of what you're already experiencing during those early months of recovery.

If you take anti-depression meds, don't stop. Speak honestly to your doctor about your plan to quit crystal meth. During this time, your serotonin and dopamine levels could use all the help they can get.

CMA and Other Programs – No One Is an Island

This book encourages you to get involved in the program of Crystal Meth Anonymous. If you live in a rural area where there are no CMA meetings, or if CMA is not right for you, you can just as easily attend the meetings of Narcotics Anonymous or, the mothership, Alcoholics Anonymous. I'll go into it in more detail—for example, on what to expect at your first meeting, how to participate or not—later. For now, I only ask that you keep an open mind to CMA and other programs.

Why?

Many reasons, but the best is this: it's at these meetings where you'll meet living, breathing examples of people who've quit successfully. At the Saturday morning "Happy, Joyous & Free" CMA meeting in Los Angeles, there are often more than fifty people in attendance with at least 2 years or more of sobriety. (Its usual size is well over one hundred recovering tweakers.) At the Thursday night CMA meeting in Palm Springs, it's not uncommon to find one or two people with over 20 years sobriety sitting in the room.

Yes, I know. Right now, 30 days seems like an eternity. But that's as it should be. I'm told it's often said at CMA meetings, "the first 30 days are the hardest." At meetings, you'll not only meet longtime survivors of meth, but more recently-recovering addicts like yourself. You can compare war stories *and* recovery stories. You will realize that your time of isolation and loneliness brought on by using can finally be at an end.

The simple truth is this: no one is an island. It's easier to quit if you have support for quitting. It's harder if you're alone. And harder still, damn near impossible, if you remain in the environment where others enable your using, instead of support your quitting.

A Few Words About Relapse

There's a lot more about relapse and recovery in this book's final chapter. But, for now, a few words are in order.

Not everyone quits on the first try. I didn't. It took me three months of seriously trying before I really, truly quit. I could give a lot of reasons, but the most honest statement about that time is: I just wasn't ready yet. I wasn't, as they say in AA, "sick and tired of being sick and tired." Despite walking on a cane with my leg swollen, I hadn't quite reached the bottom of my bottom.

But I was nearing it and knew this. So I kept trying to quit, over and over for several months, until I finally quit for real.

Relapsing is very common in the first month. That's the hardest 30 days you'll experience in your recovery. But, remember, thousands have done it before you, so you can too. The person who told you life was easy lied. Sometimes, it's difficult as hell. Sometimes, we go through relapse after relapse until we finally quit.

For others, they immediately put down the drug and the obsession is lifted—they never wish to pick up again. I hope that's true for you. But, if it's not...

Remember that relapse can be part of recovery. Especially at the beginning. Like they say in the rooms of all 12 Step programs: *just keep coming back*. Keep trying until you finally quit. It's only your life we're talking about, here. Nothing less.

Chapter 2

Withdrawal

0 – 15 Days

Withdrawal usually lasts from 1 to 2 weeks, but it can last upwards of 4 weeks—and, in some extreme cases, longer. Also known as the "sleep, eat, and drink" stage, your body and brain are in healing overdrive. There's a lot of damage meth caused that needs to be repaired before you can move forward.

For those first two weeks, all I could do
was sleep and eat, sleep and eat, and sleep
some more.

— Dana, 1 year clean

Just know you're not always going to feel
this way. Have faith that it will get better,
because it does.

— Steed, 7 years clean

WHAT TO EXPECT

The Crash – Into the Dark Void

One of the hardest parts of crystal meth withdrawal is what's called "the crash." Emotionally, it's that very dark mood coming at the end of a crystal binge—a depression characterized by sadness and hopelessness, on the one hand, and by rising anxiety or panic, on the other. Then add to this emotional hell its physical cousin, profound fatigue. Most likely, you haven't slept in many days. Most likely, you haven't been eating or hydrating properly, so it's no surprise your body craves rest and nutrition.

The crash is emotional and physical. And, other than prescribed medicines (or marijuana maintenance, which I do not suggest as a first choice), there is little you can do to alleviate the more severe symptoms other than sleeping and eating.

Just expect it. Know what's happening. Your brain's dopamine function is severely impaired right now. It may take a week or more to restore the dopamine to levels where your mood lightens, energy returns, and you have a clarity of thinking. Usually the crash lasts from three to fifteen days. But, for some longtime users, the crash may last upwards of a month or more. Remember, depending upon how long you used and how heavily, your body and brain have a lot of healing to do.

I know I was down for almost three weeks when I quit. By "down," I mean I felt like only sleeping, watching television, eating ravenously, and mostly wanting to be alone, in my bed. I forced myself to do some basic shopping

for food, and pay bills, but little else. An addict from San Francisco whom I interviewed had a history of using meth for twenty years and reported his crash lasting over three months. Whereas a housewife from the Midwest, who'd used for just under a year, swore to me her "sleepy time" lasted three days, at most. Like most meth aftereffects, the duration of the crash depends upon a host of cofactors like how much and how long you used, your age, and general health.

Here are some other common meth withdrawal symptoms: teeth grinding, jaw clenching, and night sweats. And, in the meantime, your brain will be screaming for more meth.

To successfully quit, you must ride out the crash without picking up. That's what separates the men from the boys—or, the women from the girls. Try to remember that the crash will pass and is often followed by what's called the "Honeymoon" or "Pink Cloud." This is a very uplifting and joyous part of your recovery.

So, again, the goal of these first few weeks: ride out the crash without picking up. The silver lining—that Pink Cloud—is usually right around the corner.

Eating & Appetite

You are going to feel very hungry for the simple fact you haven't eaten much over the last few days. If you don't have an appetite at first, at least hydrate. Your appetite will return shortly—and with a vengeance.

Sleeping, and More Sleeping

You are going to need to sleep a lot. This is good. You can't sleep too much during the first couple of weeks. In the beginning, it's not uncommon for days to pass where you sleep around the clock, except to get up to use the bathroom, or hurriedly eat. If you're not peeing or eating, you'll probably be sleeping. Again, depending on how heavily and long you used, your sleep-fest will last from several days to, in some cases, over a month.

This is also where your meth-addicted brain tells you that the solution to all this physical exhaustion is to pick up and use again. The temptation is extreme, especially after a few days of solid sleeping. You erroneously think: Now that I've rested a few days, if I just had that little extra bump of chemical energy, everything could get back to normal. As one addict put it, "The life I always went back to was anything but normal. I couldn't sober up

for more than a few days because I always used again so I wouldn't sleep my ass off."

The real solution here isn't more meth—it's more sleep. Remember, lots of sleep at this point of your recovery is a good thing. You can't get too much.

Confusion, Difficulty in Concentration, and Memory Loss

Depending on how heavily and long you used, you may have problems thinking and concentrating, and experience periods of confusion and memory loss. The most severe of these symptoms generally disappear as you complete detoxing. For now, just remember that *your brain is exhausted* both emotionally and biochemically.

Expect temporary confusion, difficulty in concentration and memory loss through the Withdrawal stage—and sometimes these extend, to a lesser degree, into the first few months of your recovery. Don't panic. It won't last forever. These symptoms are actually a sign that your brain is healing.

What About Hearing Voices, Feeling Paranoid, and Seeing "Tree People?"

If you regularly used high doses of crystal meth, you might develop "methamphetamine psychosis," which is a fancy way of saying your brain is temporarily sick from too much meth.

Here are some symptoms of this kind of brain sickness:

▶ seeing things or hearing voices (hallucinations);

▶ disorganized speech;

▶ feeling sensations such as bugs crawling on your skin or inside your body;

▶ elaborate paranoia—for example, the CIA, neighbors, or "tree people" are always just outside your windows, peering in.

Usually this kind of psychosis ends a few days after you've stopped using meth. But it can last weeks or, in some extreme cases, might be irreversible. And try not to panic, as these lifelong cases are very rare.

Here are some common hallucinations addicts experience: tree people, shadow people, beings lurking in your peripheral vision, voices that whisper from your attic or basement (even if you don't have an attic or basement), the sound of police helicopters approaching from the distance, aliens or ghosts speaking to you from within your television (whether it's on or not), the shuffle of invisible feet across your floor (or ceiling), the sound of that DEA or SWAT team just outside your door. You get the idea. Generally these auditory or visual hallucinations are dosed with a heavy serving of paranoia. Almost always, whatever thing you are seeing or hearing happens to be watching you too.

If you feel you are a danger to yourself or anyone else, see a doctor immediately. If you don't have a doctor, go to the emergency room. Why risk it? This way, the worst that can happen is you'll be put in the hospital on suicide-watch for a couple of days. Be sure to tell the doctor you are coming down off crystal meth, so he/she won't mistake you for run-of-the-mill paranoid schizophrenic. You are a meth addict coming off a run with too much crystal.

If you choose to ride out the hallucinations and paranoia at home, here's some information you should know:

▶ During methamphetamine psychosis your brain is hijacked and you are not in charge. The manic, paranoid tweaker in your head is running the show. And it is not to be trusted at all.

▶ The hallucinations and paranoia—the psychosis—usually ends within 2 to 3 days of quitting meth, but sometimes it can last upwards of a week or more.

▶ Finally, if your symptoms persist longer than ten days or get worse over time, call your doctor.

If you are in the midst of methamphetamine psychosis, most likely, you are not able to read these words.

If you are reading this for someone who is currently experiencing the above symptoms and has pretty much "broken from reality," you'll have to make the call for what to do. Bottom line: if you feel they may be physically dangerous to themselves or others, encourage them to go to the emergency room. And if you can't safely transport them to the hospital, call 911.

Emotional Surges – Tears, Angry Outbursts, or Both

Aside from exhaustion and a general sense of depression, you will most likely experience an emotional rollercoaster of sudden tears. Weeping at television commercials is common. A certain song plays on the radio and tears begin to fall. You are speaking to someone about something as ridiculous as the weather, but find yourself choking up with emotion. Just move through it. This is normal. It may last much of the first two weeks, or for several months.

Remember, your brain has been traumatized chemically. A lot has to happen to get your brain functions back into balance. Emotional intensity should become less over time, but it still may persist. All through my first six months, I could still tear up easily, especially when talking about my recovery or those I love.

Outbursts of anger are also very common in the first few weeks. Looking out from the darkness of the crash, it's easy to see problems everywhere and to become critical and judgmental.

One addict I interviewed during her first month of recovery told me, "If I'm not exhausted from it all, I'm so on edge I'll bite your head off. It's ridiculous and I know better, but just can't help myself. I'm constantly apologizing afterwards, which is even more exhausting."

Actually, this is the correct strategy—apologize and explain. I think it helps to prepare others for your sudden outbursts of anger. Let your friends and family know that you are angry and irritable with everything because you're going through Withdrawal. It's the side effects of the crash, not the real you, lashing out. Since your brain is not itself, apologize in advance and then try your best. Like much of this stage, it won't last too long.

Feeling Anti-Social

Most likely, the last thing you'll feel like is being social. The crash pulls you inward, into isolation. You certainly can't begin to share or empathize with others while in the first few days of recovery.

This is okay. Go easy on yourself.

Sleep, eat, and rest. Leave your important conversations until a couple of weeks have passed. Feeling anti-social during Withdrawal is perfectly normal and to be expected.

Abscesses, Staph Infections, and Meth Mouth

One addict who delayed seeing his doctor about an abscess on his arm, confessed, "Putting off the doctor was a huge mistake. Because I waited, I had to be hospitalized for two days on an IV drip." If you suspect any of your war wounds are becoming infected, or are refusing to heal within a few days, see your doctor immediately. It's foolish for you to try to handle these yourself.

The same goes for your teeth, if they are in bad shape. Don't wait. Make an appointment today—besides, it may take several days to get an appointment.

Proper treatment, dressing, and antibiotics can do wonders. We are in the 21st Century. Get some modern-day medical and dental treatment for those war wounds and you'll recover faster.

The First Month is the Hardest, Usually

It's said that one of the things you'll hear at almost any CMA meeting is: *The first 30 days are the hardest.* The best way to get through it is one day at a time. "That first month was definitely the most miserable," a lawyer from Beverly Hills told me. "I thought it'd never end. But it did." This is good advice.

"The first month is the hardest. Just get through it." If I've heard that once—or something close to it—I've heard it a hundred times. So expect this time in your recovery to be tough, but also remind yourself it'll only last a few weeks.

Here's an opposing voice to the "first month is the hardest" point of view. I've known more than one addict who said that, in less than a week, the crash lifted and they loved the first month. In fact, it was their favorite because they felt hopeful and clean of crystal for the first time in a long while. It's as if they went directly from a brief crash into a very Pink Cloud. If this is your experience, great. The less miserable your withdrawal symptoms can be, the better. Who am I to insist you have a hard first month? Just because most of us do!

Remember, the timeline of recovery is as individual as you are.

WHAT TO DO

"You just put yourself through hell.
Now it's time to love yourself."

— Maria, 5 years clean

Replenish My Body

The first thing you want to do is to break away from the "meth diet." This usually consists of Ensure, Gatorade, and the occasional protein drink every other day. Here's what you need to do.

Eat: Start eating solid foods.

Hydrate: Drink enriched water, vitamin enhanced water, or, even better, coconut water.

Get your stomach back in shape: Try probiotic drinks like Kefir and yogurt. I especially recommend Yakult, a great product from Japan available in most major chain grocery stores.

Vitamins: Take a multi-vitamin daily. Maybe double up for a week. Also increase your potassium intake. Probably the best source is coconut water, but there are always bananas.

And, of course, the next best thing you can do for your body is to rest. Sleep, sleep, and more sleep. Let your body recover from the intense run you've just been on.

Calm My Mind

As with replenishing your body, resting is very important. This means not only sleep, but you also might want to rest your mind by "zoning out" with a marathon of your favorite TV shows or movies. "Thank God for streaming Netflix," one addict told me. "I spent my entire Withdrawal watching hours and hours of *Glee*."

Basically, you're just trying to get through the next week or two without stressing your body and mind any more than they already are. In this detox phase of your recovery, you may be depressed and, most likely, highly emotional. Your brain is desperately trying to heal right now. Try to give it a break and just zone out with something mindless from time to time.

And if you are quitting under the care of a doctor, she or he can tell if you need Ativan or Klonopin (and will prescribe a *limited* amount) to help calm you from the immediate physical and emotional distress of withdrawal.

Banish Shame

It's natural to feel ashamed of the mess your life has become because of this disease. But, if you are to survive, you're going to have to jettison any shame, at least for the time being. After you've moved through the initial stages of recovery, you will be able to address the damage you've done and find other ways to move forward responsibly.

For today, try to remember you have a disease. Your brain is still physically malfunctioning and *it's going to take time to heal*. It is crucial that you give yourself this time. Feeling shame can keep you in a loop—or shame spiral—where, instead of moving forward with healthy recovery, you become overwhelmed with guilt and keep relapsing. For the sake of your sobriety, you must banish shame from your life today.

Here's the blunt fact: shame is the great enemy of recovery, in both the short and long term.

Do Not Make Any Big Decisions

Now is not the time to make any of those "big" life decisions. In fact, you can't trust your decision-making process at this point because your brain is a mess.

Now is *not* the time to quit your job or end a relationship. Now is *not* the time to come clean to grandma about your addiction. Now is *not* the time to confess anything to anyone, period.

Just sleep, rest, and eat—for now.

Set a Sobriety Date

Figure out the date on which you were first clean and sober. I began counting mine at the beginning of my crash, after 24 hours had passed since I'd last used crystal. There are some cool phone apps for this. Search for "sobriety" at your app store.

Though some people don't like to count days, I think it's important—especially in early recovery. Just remember, in the first few weeks, every day is a big deal. Don't fret, it won't be this hard forever.

Counting your clean days is a good way to bolster your sobriety. The days will add up quicker than you think. And they're witness to the hard work you're doing to get and stay clean.

Chapter 3

The Honeymoon

Days 16 – 45 (up to 8 Weeks)

The crash has lifted, your body has made those immediately needed repairs, and you are feeling physically and emotionally much stronger. You might even feel great, better than you've felt in years. And it's only the beginning of the third week! Unfortunately, this upswing can lead to overconfidence and you might find yourself minimizing your past meth problem.

A lot of people will relapse here because of this overconfidence. But not you. You are prepared. You understand this Honeymoon won't last. Still, there's much to enjoy while it does.

And much to do in the meantime, while you're feeling stronger.

Finally, it gets a lot better.

— Ruth, 3 years clean

I have to remind myself: I have the only
disease in the world that tries to talk me
out of having it. It's constantly telling me,
"You're better now. You can control yourself
and party just one more time."

— John, 3 years clean

WHAT TO EXPECT

The Pink Cloud

"After about a week of feeling awful and sleeping all day, I woke up feeling great. It was like a light switch had been thrown in my brain and body. I had hope and energy back. I even found myself humming while taking a shower. I really felt the obsession to use had been lifted. I was suddenly so glad to be alive. I'd forgotten how great just an ordinary day can be." These words were said to me by an addict just one month into recovery and are an example of the "Pink Cloud," as the old-timers from AA say. It's a great time in your recovery and not everyone experiences it in such dramatic terms. Still, for most of us, this "Honeymoon" from our addiction happens to one degree or another.

Why? Again, the answer is biochemical and has to do with the brain. It usually takes a week or two to replenish the dopamine in your brain to acceptable levels. When that happens, your mood lightens and energy returns, along with some clarity of thinking. Liberated from your meth obsession, everything can seem suddenly happy, rosy, and wonderful. Hence the name, Pink Cloud.

Whether or not you experience this elation in all its glory depends on your individual brain chemistry. For some, there is no wide pendulum swing over to a big fluffy Pink Cloud. There's merely a feeling that life isn't as utterly hopeless as it seemed during the Crash. It's not as dramatic, but there's a definite upswing out of despair and exhaustion.

For most, the Pink Cloud lasts about a month. So, enjoy it. Now is a time to dive headlong into recovery. There are a lot of things to do at this stage in your recovery and we'll look at those in the next section "What to Do."

Use that newfound energy to go to CMA meetings, make new friends, and establish new routines and ways of living that support your sobriety. Put that Pink Cloud to good use and get fully active in your recovery. For now, however, there are some other things to expect during this Honeymoon period...

Dreams of Using Meth

You will probably begin to have "using dreams" during this time. I had about a dozen in the first four months. You may have many, or few. The first thing most people report from these dreams is that they awake feeling guilty—as if they actually used. That's normal. But after the momentary blip of guilt, try to feel immense gratitude for the reality that you didn't use. It was only a dream, thank God.

Dreams of using don't mean you're headed on the fast track to relapse. Dreams are your unconscious working out deeper issues.

If you want to dwell on these dreams, try looking at what else was going on besides your using. Who else was in the room with you? Did you hesitate before picking up? Or gleefully partake? Just note it—maybe write it down so you'll remember. Then, the next time you have a using dream, note how this changes. What is your dream telling you about how you *feel* about using, about what's happening *around* the use? This is far richer territory to explore.

Almost a year into my recovery, I dreamed I was offered a pipe and then I turned it down, got up and left the situation. When I awoke it was such a great dream to remember. My using dream was a not-using dream.

Most likely, you will eventually have not-using dreams yourself.

Memory Loss May Get Worse at First

During the early weeks after quitting meth, you may have trouble remembering things. Your memory may even seem to be getting worse. The good news is, depending on how long and how much you used, most of your memory will return after the first couple of months. Though some recovering addicts with long-term, heavy use report permanent memory issues, brain imaging has shown that this damage is usually reversible over time.

So, hang in there. Most likely your memory will start to get much better after a month or two.

What About Numbness from Injection Sites?

If you slammed your meth, you may have places on your arms or hands where you "missed" the vein and injected meth into body tissue by mistake. A small, hard knot often forms at these missed injection sites. The knot usually dissolves in a month or so, but you can quicken this process by applying heat—a heating pad or hot compress—so the capillaries will absorb the chemical residue into the bloodstream at a faster rate.

After the knot breaks, a patch of your skin and the tissue beneath it usually goes numb. How big the numb patch is and how long it will last depends upon how much meth was injected and, of course, the potency of the batch. Again, it's important to understand this numbness can last up to four months. Don't freak out if these patches of numbness take a while to dissipate, but they eventually go away. Try to have patience.

Triggers and Cravings

A song comes on the radio that you first heard while using. Or a person you once partied with walks out of the grocery store as you arrive. It can be as innocent as the straw a waitress sets next to your iced tea. Any of these people, places or things can trigger memories from your "old" life when you used. These memories—called *triggers*—usually lead to other *thoughts* about using. This thinking about using often evokes a longing that leads to a *craving*, an intense feeling in which you suddenly want or need the drug. If unchecked, *using* is often not far behind.

The sequence is: *Trigger… Thought… Craving… Use.*

Triggers are everywhere. You'll learn them, and then learn to avoid them when appropriate. For instance, the smell of bleach for one addict triggered memories of bathhouses and drug-fueled sex parties, so for the first year of his recovery he had to get rid of all the bleach in his apartment. For people who smoked cigarettes while high, smoking can be a troublesome trigger. The good news is that triggers often become less potent over time. The certain song that, in your first month, sent you into a mad craving tizzy may, after several more months, lose its power over you. With time, the potency of your triggers and the cravings usually mellow.

Successfully quitting meth has a lot to do with learning how to check these cravings and interrupt the sequence of Trigger-Thought-Craving-Use. (We'll look at some good strategies for this is the next section of this chapter, "What To Do.") For now, just know these triggers and cravings are to be expected. Don't worry—they can be dealt with successfully without relapsing. The fact is triggers and cravings are part of recovery.

WHAT TO DO

Remember: My Disease Wants Me Dead

A good way to think about your addiction is to personalize it. Think of your addiction as a living being, as "my disease," who has wants and desires. Whenever you get triggered, remind yourself that the "thought of using" is your "disease speaking" within your mind. And remember, "My disease wants to kill me." This motto or a variation of it—like, *My disease wants me dead*—can be a powerful affirmation whenever thoughts turn toward using.

In AA, people often say, "I'm fine while in the meeting. It's when I get to my car afterwards I'm in trouble. While I was sitting calmly inside, my disease was doing pushups out in the parking lot." I like this because it reminds me that, at any moment, even when the last thing on my mind is using, this disease can rear its ugly head. Try considering any using thoughts as the voice of your disease—a malevolent "other" who is out to harm you. This is closer to the truth than not.

Your disease has a lot of great lies to tell about how, now that you're a few weeks sober, you can use meth in a "controlled" way. Also, this disease is one of the few diseases in the world that tries to convince you that you don't have it. It says to your thoughts, again and again, "Your not a real addict. You can control your using, if you really want to."

It would be laugh out loud funny if it weren't so deadly.

It's crucial to realize your disease wants one thing, to kill you. During my first year, I said to myself at least once a day: "My disease wants only one thing, to kill me."

Keep the Goal of Quitting, Today

For some addicts, holding on to the idea that they are quitting "forever" is very important—we need that big goal. I am one such addict. To quit, I needed the grand promise that I was quitting forever, that my using days were definitely over and behind me. Crystal was to be banished from my life henceforth! If this works for you, great. Hold up that big prize and keep it in sight.

But not everyone thinks this way. And, even if you do, there will most likely be moments during your early recovery when you really crave a hit of meth.

At times like these, it might not help to think about quitting "forever." Here, it's better to think *in terms of days, sometimes even minutes or hours.* Come on, not using for a day is a lot easier than not using for a month!

Sometimes it pays to keep your goal of quitting small and easier to reach.

Don't set yourself up for failure if "quitting forever" seems too overwhelming. When I had a craving in my first few months, I would promise myself that, if I still had the craving tomorrow, I'd use then. Here was the bargain: I merely needed to postpone using today until tomorrow and *then* I could have one last party. (And I was serious—it was a real promise.) At first, this sounds like a recipe for relapse, right? Here's what happened. Every time without fail, when tomorrow came, I felt one thing—immense gratitude that I didn't use the day before.

Keep the goal of quitting small when you need to, but keep the goal of quitting for today.

Keep Other Small, Daily Goals

The goal of quitting is always first and foremost. Don't use. But you'll need other goals along the journey, daily goals you can accomplish and check off as you achieve them. Maybe one goal is to start going to the gym, and another to start some creative project like learning to paint or write, or bake.

Here are a few good small, daily goals for early recovery: *To stay awake all day* so that, at night, you begin to normalize sleep. *To walk briskly for 20 minutes out of doors. To sit in quiet meditation for 10 minutes*, a time you can lengthen as you get better at it. *To call three sober friends today* just to say hello, get out of your own head, and ask how their day is going.

It's important to make these goals small so that you can actually accomplish them. Remember, your primary goal is always: *to stay clean of crystal*. So, your other smaller goals should take a backseat. But, it's important to have them.

One of the primary reasons for relapse is boredom. You need to have goals that keep you busy. Keep other goals, but small goals.

Normalize Sleep and Routine

During withdrawal, the idea of needing medication to help you sleep is laughable. You're exhausted and have no trouble conking out. But as you move into the next month or so, you may begin to notice that, though you have no trouble napping in the middle of the afternoon, you do have trouble sleeping the entire night through. Anxiety and insomnia are often common nighttime experiences during these weeks. So it's important to normalize sleep as soon as you can.

You want to get off that "meth schedule" of staying up all night and catching a few hours, if any, during the day. You want to get back into the routine of the regular non-using world that sleeps at night and is awake during daylight hours. Normalizing your sleep allows you to focus on what's most important in day-to-day life.

Sleeping medication. Talk to your doctor if you want Trazodone, a nonaddictive powerfully sedating antidepressant, which is commonly prescribed for sleep. Personally, I like over-the-counter Benadryl. It tends to knock me out about an hour after I take it and I can sleep a good six hours. But there are all kinds of meds for sleeping and it's best to ask your doctor.

It is suggested that you do NOT take: Ambien, Sonata, and Lunesta which are "benzo-like" medications that target the same brain receptors as benzodiazepines. They are too easily abused and when taken in larger doses can cause psychotic symptoms, such as hallucinations. Been there, done that.

Again, ask your doctor's advice, but definitely tell him/her you don't want the "benzo-like" medications. Your doctor should know you are a recovering addict and prescribe appropriate medicines.

Recognize Triggers

Just about everything else you read in this chapter is going to be about how to avoid obvious triggers and/or counteract cravings. There are two kinds of triggers.

External triggers. These are things outside yourself that trigger a using thought. Like a text from an old using buddy. Or a certain online hookup site. Or the neighborhood where your dealer lived. We'll look at a few of the obvious ones and give you strategies to avoid them later in this chapter.

Internal triggers. These are triggers that originate from within you, usually emotions. Some people are triggered to use when very sad or depressed. You just want the low to be wiped away by the euphoria of the drug. Others, myself included, get triggered by just the opposite—joy and excitement. When something good happens, my disease tells me: "This is so great! Let's get high to celebrate and make this greatness last longer!" Some people are triggered when they feel misunderstood, criticized or ignored. Others when they get deeply angered, irritated, or feel embarrassed. Just about any strong emotion can be a trigger for you to use—if you associate using with it. Discover which emotional states trigger you the strongest.

Here is an important way to deal with any trigger...

Stop the Thought

Earlier in this chapter, we learned the sequence of *Trigger-Thought-Craving*. It goes like this: First, something *triggers* you to remember a time when you used. Next, you have *more thoughts* about using, perhaps glamorizing the party. This leads directly to the *craving*, that intense feeling where you want or feel the need to use now.

One successful strategy is to "stop the thought" dead in its tracks before you arrive at the craving. You interrupt the sequence before the thought of using can turn into a full-fledged craving. There are many ways to do this and I encourage you to find those that work best for you.

Here are some ideas:

Visualize the "thought" as a TV screen image, then change the channel. Picture the image of that using thought on a TV screen inside your mind. Then visualize yourself changing the channel of that inner TV. Pick a positive, happy image for the new channel—say, the image of someone you love dearly, hugging you. Or your favorite view of the ocean. Something powerful that instantly elicits happy feelings. So, you visualize this channel switch in your mind, and the new positive image appears on that inner TV screen.

Think of something that evokes a powerful emotion, like anger—but has no associations with using. One recovering addict told me he "stopped

the thought" by immediately thinking of a certain politician who made him furious. Just rekindling his anger toward this politician (or political party) was enough to get his mind completely off using for the moment. Who knew politics could be put to such good use? (And, obviously, if anger is one of your triggers, you shouldn't try this.)

Snap that rubber band on your wrist. If the stop-the-thought process isn't working for you, try a preplanned action that interrupts the thought. Some rehab centers advise you to wear a rubber band around your wrist so that, whenever you catch yourself thinking about meth, you can snap the rubber band. This jogs your thinking process and stops the forward momentum toward craving and use. The sting of the rubber band on your wrist brings your thoughts back to the present moment.

But, say, you've moved past the thinking/glamorizing stage and are feeling a full-fledged craving. Here are some ways to counteract that craving once it's begun...

Counteract the Craving

The good news first: cravings will last only 30-90 seconds unless you start moving toward drug use. If you can wait it out, or counteract the craving, it will pass soon enough.

Say, you are triggered or have a pleasurable flashback, here are several ways to counteract the craving that follows:

Tell someone about it, now. Don't wait till later. Pick up the phone and call your "besty" or sponsor now. Get a phone list from a CMA or NA meeting and start calling until someone answers. They will be happy to be of service.

Play the memory forward to the bitter end. Don't just think about the euphoria of initially getting high. Jump ahead and play the memory forward to the bitter end. Remember how you felt *at the end* of your run. Remember those unsavory people with whom you were partying by the final days. Remember the desperation and loneliness. One recovering addict told me, whenever she had a using fantasy or craving, she immediately remembered that last week of using before she quit. Instead of having euphoric recall, she had "horrific recall." Remembering and re-feeling the horror of that last week of using was enough to bring her mind back into right thinking.

Go to a CMA or AA/NA Meeting ASAP. Don't wait till later. Go to the very next meeting. Just sit there quietly in the safety, or share. The main thing is to surround yourself with sobriety, as soon as possible. If there isn't a CMA

meeting near, try NA. Also, in most cities, there is an AA meeting happening somewhere within the next two hours.

Surf the Urge. Cravings are a lot like wave swells in the ocean. They get bigger as they approach the shoreline, eventually reach a peak, then slide back into calm water. Another good technique to counteract a craving is to imagine yourself riding atop it like a surfer on a wave. You don't get down into the craving, but stay on the surface and ride the wave beneath you. Other thoughts will soon take over and, in 60 to 90 seconds, you'll be onto another thought. Imagine yourself surfing atop the urge until the wave dissipates and slides back into the calm.

Keep Your Feet Moving. If you can get through the moment, the desire to use will pass. Don't sit there stewing in the feeling/craving. Get up and get your feet moving. *Move physically and you will move emotionally.* Here's a short list of things you can do to take your mind off a craving: go to the gym, go to a coffee shop, force yourself to talk to a stranger, see a movie, play a highly-interactive video game, go dancing with a friend, take a brisk walk. The point is to get up, get moving, and distract your mind with a new be-havior—those moving feet—instead of allowing that feeling/craving to turn into the old behavior of using.

These are just a few ways to counteract a craving. The main goal is always to truncate the craving—interrupt it with some learned, new behavior—before the desire to use becomes overwhelming.

Now, here are some proactive things to do in order to avoid triggers and minimize cravings beforehand...

Change Phone Number and Contact Info

The single best thing you can do for your recovery is to change your phone number. The next best thing you can do is change your email or, if you had a separate account for your using, delete it altogether. You don't want your old using buddies to be able to contact you. You want to leave them behind with that old life.

Delete All Using Contacts

You may think deleting old using contacts, including your dealer's, is some-thing to be done before quitting. If you can do any of this beforehand, great. But, for many of us, we can't actually do these absolutely necessary actions until

after we begin our recovery in full. That's why they are placed here, within the timeline of the first few weeks.

All those old using contacts need to be deleted. The dealers, the party buddies, the project tweakers. All erased so that you can't retrieve them. And don't forget to delete the phone numbers in your call history, as well.

Delete Social Media, Too

Sex hookup sites. Craigslist. Even Facebook. All social media that you employed in your using career need to be deleted. If your Facebook is overwhelmed with using buddies, create a wholly new account and send friend requests only to your non-using friends. Then delete your old accounts altogether.

Putting your hookup sites on "hold" or merely adding "HELL NO" to drugs or "NO PNP," is a slippery slope. It's best to delete your old profile, with all your old buddy lists, at once. If you keep your old username and all the partying buddies on your favorite list, what's the point?

If you are serious about your sobriety, you *must* delete your old party hookup accounts. *Don't do this alone.* Have a sober friend sit with you as you delete the accounts. Avoid the temptation to check the last emails and notices, just cancel your accounts altogether.

Only later, once you are many months into your recovery, or whenever you feel it's right, create a new account as a sober person. State in your profile that you are "in recovery" and "absolutely no partying or drugs." In short, give yourself some time away from the internet at the start of your quitting.

Nothing can take a person out quicker than an offer to party with a hot hookup. So don't let it get that far. Avoid all social media that intersected with your using and create new accounts that are for your sober life and friends.

When You Get a Call or Text from an Old Using Friend

If for some reason you can't change your number—and it needs to be a *very* good reason—here are some steps you can take:

Don't answer any unrecognized number. Once you delete all your using contacts from your phone and computer, don't answer any calls that come through with only a number identification—it's probably an old using buddy. Let all unknown callers go to voice mail. Screen your calls.

Respond by texting only. So a using friend calls and leaves a message. Don't call back and speak to them. Respond with a text. Something like: "I no

longer party. It was affecting my health. I wish you well. Peace." Keep it short, sweet, and *do not invite a response*.

Delete incoming and outgoing phone and text histories. Don't forget to delete any record of that call/text from your using friend. Be vigilant about this. You don't want their number to be stored anywhere that you can find later. Remember to delete both incoming and outgoing histories. Thinking that you don't have to delete this history is actually setting the stage for relapse.

Change Old Patterns & Routines

Old hangouts of your using days should be avoided now that you are clean. Find a new coffee shop if you met your dealer at the old one. If you live in a state that allows over-the-counter syringe purchases, go to a different pharmacy, one where you've not purchased points. Do you regularly run into old using buddies at a local grocery or convenience store? Then it's time to change these routines. Do you pass a house you used to party in as you drive to work? Change your route to work, even if it means taking a longer way. You are trying to change any old patterns and routines that might trigger a craving.

Perhaps you always listened to a certain radio station when you were high. I went through a two month period where I couldn't listen to any dance mixes because it took my mind immediately back to using.

If you drank Gatorade and sports drinks while you partied, switch to brands you never used, or to more healthy alternatives like vitamin-enriched or coconut waters. Certainly avoid that particular 24-hour McDonalds you always tweaked at. Try another McDonalds. (Or maybe something better for your body like Subway.) You may find you have to change a lot of your routine. This is okay.

You are changing your life. It's no small order.

It won't always be like this. When I lived in Los Angeles, I used to drive near my dealer's house a couple of times a week. There was just no way around it. I'd obsess about it as I neared the intersection, then hold my breath as I passed. This went on for about four months into my sobriety. Then one Sunday morning, I ate lunch with friends at a restaurant right around the corner and didn't realize I was a block from my old dealer's apartment until walking back to my car. I'd spent and entire hour within a hundred yards of the room I'd bought and used in for months—and none of this crossed my mind. I just ate

lunch and enjoyed the time with friends. So your triggers do change, do lessen over time. That's the good news.

Move (or Redecorate)

If you used heavily in your neighborhood, move as soon as you can. And don't move into another neighborhood where you also used. That defeats the purpose. Bottom line: if you can move from the place you used in to another apartment, another neighborhood, or even city, do it.

If you can't change your living situation, the next best thing is to redecorate. I'm serious. Especially change up your bedroom, if you often used there. Make your new non-using environment wholly different from that place where you used meth. A new coat of paint, a rearranging of furniture, new bedspread—all this works wonders. You are trying to lessen the triggers you encounter on a daily basis. Start with your living space.

Also, the same goes for any space where you once used. If you used in an office at work, rearrange that office. The goal is to create life anew.

Find a Besty With Whom I Can Be Completely Honest

When triggered, one of the best things you can do to counteract it is to "tell on yourself." That means talk about it with someone—give them the gory details of your flashback, craving or fantasy. You'll be amazed at how confessing to a craving will lessen its power over you. For your sobriety, it's crucial that you find a best friend with whom you can be completely honest.

If you are working a CMA program, this person will be your sponsor. But even though you tell your sponsor everything, I think it's good to have another sober friend with whom you can come clean. The more sober friends you have who understand, the better. When we keep our urges to use secret, we're far more likely to relapse.

One evening, out of nowhere, the thought crossed my mind that on my next trip into Los Angeles, I could have a one-night party. (After all, I'd been sober over six months at that point, didn't I deserve a little reward?) So within ten seconds, I planned what lie I would tell my friends in Palm Springs, the lies I'd tell to my L.A. friends who thought I was coming to visit, planned exactly where I'd stay to party, from whom I'd buy the drugs (online) and exactly how much I would pay for an eight ball. Really. In a

matter of seconds. My monkey mind ran with it, planned the whole thing out.

In maybe ten more seconds, I was floored by guilt. Immediately, I extended the thought to include how awful the end of the party would be, how I'd feel when I crashed the day after—then I realized, who was I kidding? I'd never partied for just one night in my life. My usual run was 3 to 5 days, always 5 toward the end. No, if I used, I'd party 5 days then crash briefly and rationalize that, since I've lost my sobriety already, I might as well party for a while longer. And so the cycle begins. I might go on another year-long run, or worse. When my mind played thorough this possibility I was relieved because the urge to use, the sudden fantasy, had been busted. Still, I knew what I had to do.

The next morning, I took two sober friends aside and confessed the whole thing to take away any power that it might hold if I kept it secret. I eventually shared about it at a group level later in the week, disempowering the fantasy even more. Having a friend, or several, you can share everything with is crucial to sobriety. Because we have to learn not to shame ourselves when our disease rears its ugly head. It's not a weakness of character to be triggered or get lost in a using fantasy. It's what the malfunctioning brain of an addict does—craves more drugs.

How we treat that craving is the key. Don't keep it secret. Take away your disease's power over you by "telling on yourself."

Practice an Elevator Pitch for Saying "No"

In Hollywood, the "elevator pitch" is that short and sweet sales pitch (usually for a film) that is succinct, well-practiced and to the point. You always have your pitch at the ready, in case you happen to find yourself standing one day next to Steven Spielberg in an elevator.

For you, the elevator pitch is that immediate and practiced response you'll give to someone who offers you meth. This particularly applies to people from your using days who you might encounter on the street, at the grocery store, online, or even in an elevator.

Whenever asked if you want to party, give your elevator pitch immediately and without reservation. Here are some examples for you to tinker with and make your own:

"No, thanks. I no longer party. Crystal almost destroyed my life. So, again, no."

"No. I really have a problem with crystal and have decided to stop. As my friend, I know you'll understand. So please don't talk to me about it again."

"No, thanks. Crystal was really messing with my health, so I'm not partying any more."

Find your own elevator pitch and *memorize it*. Then you must PRACTICE YOUR PITCH, saying it forcefully and without reservation.

Practice, practice, practice. Imagine various scenarios where someone asks you to use with them, and practice saying your pitch. This is a great exercise to do with sober friends. Role play and take turns pretending to be that favorite dealer you've accidentally met on the Gatorade aisle at Albertsons. Take turns asking each other if you'd like to use, then practice your response. Get really good at your "no, thanks" pitch.

This way, if the situation occurs where someone offers you crystal, you'll instantly respond with a well-practiced elevator pitch that flows quickly off your tongue.

And then get the hell out of that elevator, fast.

Schedule a Dental Exam

Here's one of the single most important gifts you can give yourself in sobriety. As meth addicts, we usually have very bad dental hygiene. Do it now. Call and make that appointment.

Get Professional Help – Drug Counseling vs. Traditional Therapy

If you can work with a therapist or counselor who specializes in addiction, consider getting some professional help, as well. This is not the time for "traditional" psychotherapy, however. Now is *not* the time to dig into yesteryear's childhood traumas to understand how they affect your relationships today. Instead, now is the time to focus on relapse prevention skills, on how to cope with cravings, and avoid triggers and so on. While understanding your troubled childhood may be important in the longer run, it's not helpful now and may even be harmful.

In these early months of recovery, you don't need the additional stress involved in deep, exploratory therapy. Quitting crystal and learning how to

keep clean is the task for today. And, believe me, that's enough. Save the deeper inquiries for later.

Ideally, you would want a drug counselor/therapist who is experienced in working with crystal meth users. But if you can't find one in your area, a general addiction counselor can still be helpful to your growth. The basic problems of addiction are universal regardless of the drug. Today you need someone in your corner who understands addictive behaviors and is trained to help you overcome them.

The difference between a counselor and a traditional therapist is: a counselor will tell you what to do; a therapist will listen to you. At this point in your recovery you need to be told what to do. (If you seek out a therapist now, as opposed to a drug counselor, I recommend you find a therapist who specializes in dialectical behavior therapy or cognitive behavior therapy with an emphasis in drug recovery.)

You had bad habits when you were using. You were accustomed to zero structure. But in your recovery, you'll need to form good habits. Counselors teach good habits and they teach you structure. And, most importantly, they teach you to believe that structure is a good and safe thing.

Attend a CMA Meeting

Last, but certainly not least, one great way to help you stay clean is to start going to CMA meetings. I've heard it said by more than one recovering addict that, in their first few weeks, it was only when at a meeting that they felt calm, only then did their mind stop racing. In the early weeks of recovery, you might find that meetings offer the same calming effect for you.

The next chapter explores the pros and cons of CMA meetings and tells you what you can expect if you go to one. So please keep an open mind. And now, everything you always wanted to know about CMA but were afraid to ask...

Chapter 4

CMA Meetings

What It's All About

The simple truth is this: It's easier to quit if you have support for quitting. It's harder if you're alone. And harder still, damn near impossible, if you remain in the environment where others enable your using, instead of supporting your quitting.

Get to a meeting. Take a desire chip. Get a
sponsor.

— Theo, 15 years clean

There's a saying we have in AA and CMA. It
goes, "Meeting-makers make it." I used to
turn my nose up at that one, but over this
last year, I've watched four people with
longtime sobriety go back out. And I mean
longtime sobriety, each having well over
five years. The one thing they all shared
in common? Each had stopped going to
meetings on a regular basis. Life was just
too successful and full that they no longer
found time to prioritize a meeting within
their weekly schedule.

— Deborah, 8 years clean

It is so okay to ask for help. I didn't think it
was at first and I was wrong. Ask for help.
How else are you going to get it?

— Carol, 7 years

WHY THESE MEETINGS?

The Pros

You might not be a "crowd person" or "joiner," but it doesn't matter. You certainly don't have to be either to get great benefit from a CMA meeting. Here are some pros:

You'll meet living, breathing people who have been successful in quitting. This lets you know that, in fact, quitting is possible. It's not just a theory, but reality. Also, if you have any questions about your recovery that this book doesn't cover, most likely you'll find an answer from someone who has gone through it before.

A meeting is a great place to make new non-using friends. Where else are you going to have a room full of people who are like you, addicts trying to quit? Most likely a using friend is one of your triggers. But the new friends you make at meetings should support you in trying to quit.

You'll be able to "speak out" those thoughts you bottle up about using and recovery. It's at meetings where you'll meet someone who's gone through what you're currently experiencing—say, you just had a using dream and are feeling guilty because you enjoyed it. You can commiserate or, at the least, have a sympathetic ear. Also, "telling on yourself"—for instance, telling aloud about that impulse you had yesterday to phone your dealer, or whatever—is a great way to take your power back from your disease. Your meth addiction wants you to keep many secrets. It's those secrets that will often take the newcomer out again.

If you have something you need to share, but don't want to do it on a group level, then pick someone who has some time under their belt and go up to them

after the meeting and say, "I really need to talk. Would you be willing to listen?" Most likely, they will be honored.

The Cons

It's rare that it happens, but the biggest downside to a CMA meeting is the same danger you have whenever you get a group of newly sober tweakers together—the possibility that someone might ask you to use with them. I've never had anyone offer me meth at a meeting, but I know it's happened. And though you can be asked to use anytime anywhere, a group of newly sober addicts are particularly vulnerable. Again, it will probably never happen to you, but it's the dark little secret that needs to be talked about. The meeting should be a sacred space, but the reality is predators exist. I've even known of a dealer who once came to a meeting in search of new clients. So remember, though the room is filled with a lot of solid sobriety, it's also peppered with struggling addicts. Just a concern to keep in mind.

Other, lesser cons...

Some newcomers complain they feel "left out" because almost every person in the room already knows everyone. They greet with kisses or hugs, calling out to one another by name. Of course, the upside is that, if you stay around, soon you'll be one of the people who gets hugged and called by name too. Meetings challenge you to get out of yourself, take risks, and meet new people.

If you are terminally shy, it will be more difficult. But only more difficult, not impossible. And, once you introduce yourself, you'll never find a group of more accepting people.

Another common newcomer complaint is: "These meetings depress me because people whine and bellyache so much." There's always an excuse for what's wrong with a meeting. Too many people. Not enough people. Too many tweakers. No tweakers, just a lot of AA drunks and me. Too many people share. Not enough people share. And so on. It's at times like this when it helps to remind yourself: *I have the one of the few diseases in the world that tries to convince me that I don't have it.* The disease in your mind is working overtime telling you: "I don't belong here at this meeting, with these people."

Remember, your disease wants you to keep away from meetings at all costs. It wants you to avoid all the things that are good for your recovery. It desperately wants to convince you that you are now well and can party responsibly, just on weekends—you know, like you did once, a long time ago. It'll come up with a lot of excuses to keep you away from 12 Step meetings.

Other Fellowships – AA and NA

For various reasons, you might not be able to go to a CMA meeting. Perhaps there's not one in your area or, say, it meets only once a week. Or, perhaps, being in a room full of former tweakers is too triggering for you.

I've met a few addicts who couldn't go to CMA meetings because they always left the meeting with cravings. Something about the meeting triggered them profoundly. If this is you, then AA or NA (Narcotics Anonymous) will work better. Though, after enough time has passed and you're not so easily triggered, you might want to try CMA again. There's nothing like a room full of "your people" to make you realize you're not in this journey of recovery alone.

Isolation is the big enemy.

Every successfully recovered addict I know will tell you, almost immediately, they didn't do it alone—in fact, they couldn't have done it without the support of friends or "the fellowship" of CMA, NA, or AA.

A word about AA: Most AA meetings ask that you identify solely as an "alcoholic," period. They ask that you keep your "meth addict" identity to yourself. This is because, in the early days before CMA or NA, many AA meetings were overrun by addicts seeking help. I know many tweakers who go to AA meetings and in their mind substitute "meth addict" for alcoholic. You'll find the similarities between the meth addict and the alcoholic are many and the differences few.

Just attending the meeting is the important thing. You're in a room with people who understand, people quitting along with you. A meeting reminds you, you are not alone.

WHAT TO EXPECT AT A MEETING

"Hello, my name is X, and I'm a crystal meth addict."

These are the words that open every CMA meeting. The leader introduces himself or herself and then self-identifies as a crystal meth addict. At one point near the beginning of the meeting, introductions will go around the room and each person announces some version of "I'm [name] and I'm a crystal meth addict." Or "tweaker." Or sometimes just "addict," especially if the person has other drug programs they're working. It's also fine to simply say, "[your name], meth addict." When there's a large room, sometimes brevity is appreciated, though not required.

The only requirement for attending a CMA meeting is the desire to quit using crystal meth. Period.

If you can't go alone, you can always have a friend go with you. If your friend is not an addict, he or she can simply self-identify as: "I'm [name] and I'm here to support [your name]."

The Typical CMA Meeting

Most CMA meetings last one hour and follow a similar format. It always opens with the leader for the meeting—there's usually a different guest leader every week—announcing, "Hello, my name is X and I'm a crystal meth addict." That's when the group answers back, in unison, "Hello, X." Often the meeting continues with the Serenity Prayer.

Then the leader usually adds, "I have identified myself as a crystal meth addict. Are there any other crystal meth addicts present?"

This is when everyone in the room raises a hand. As a group, we all self-identify as crystal meth addicts. You don't have to say anything here, only raise your hand. (If you can't raise your hand, that's okay, too. But you are a meth addict, so why not?) There's tremendous power in self-identifying. You take power back from your disease, an illness that demanded secrecy from you for so long. You are no longer ashamed.

Often, this is when the leader announces: "If there are any newcomers who are in their first 30 days of sobriety, please raise your hand and state the nature of your disease. We do this not to embarrass you, but so we can get to know you better."

Now you can either raise your hand and self-identify with "I'm [your name] and I'm a meth addict" or not. Sometimes it's just too overwhelming to self-identify. Often when you first start going to meetings you just want to sit in the back and participate minimally. That's fine. There are no rules on "how to" attend. But I would encourage you to raise your hand and tell the room you are a newcomer. Because, the only way you are going to start making new non-using friends at meetings is to identify yourself—and newcomers get special attention, because we all remember how difficult it is to go through those first 30 days.

Next usually comes the "Selected Readings" portion of the meeting. Examples of these readings are "Am I a Tweaker?," "The 12 Steps and How They Work," and "What is the CMA Program?" These readings are usually printed on laminated sheets handed out to different people before the meeting begins. So it's possible you might be asked to read aloud one of these when you first attend. (It's considered an honor—no one is trying to put you on the spot.) Just know you can always say, "Thank you, but I'm new and I'd rather just watch for now." No one wants to make you feel uncomfortable.

Important to know: You can always say, "I pass," if asked to do anything that you don't want to do, like share or read aloud.

The selected readings usually last from five to ten minutes. Listen to them. This will tell you much about CMA and its philosophy.

Then sometime, either early or late in the meeting, the group observes what's called "the seventh tradition"—which states that all CMA groups must be self supporting. This is when a basket gets passed for donations. A dollar is plenty. Also, it's more than acceptable to just pass along the basket without putting in any money. Many people do. If you go to one or more meetings a day – sometimes people go to two or three – it can get too expensive to put a

dollar in the basket each time. No one should judge you. This basket is also where you will drop your Court Cards or Sober House Cards, to be signed by the secretary, if you have these.

Fairly soon, within 15 minutes of the start of the meeting, you'll get to the speaker portion. At a meeting where the speaker has 30 minutes or more to talk, you'll often hear their whole recovery story—from what it used to be like in their using days, to what happened to make them quit, to what it's like for them now in recovery. The better meetings tend to focus more on the recovery side of our stories, but hearing the horror tales repeated every once in a while is a good reminder of how awful life was when using.

Some meetings only let the speaker share from 5 to 10 minutes. It just depends on the meeting. After the speaker finishes, the meeting is opened to general participation. That means you can raise your hand and the leader, usually, will call on a person to share. If you don't raise your hand, you don't have to speak. (The only exception is a "round robin" meeting, and these will be identified in the meeting schedule. In a round robin everyone, around the room, shares for a limited time. It's a good type of meeting to go to if you are shy and want to force yourself to share.) Most meetings have a 3-5 minute limit on sharing. Sometimes a person holds a timer, just in case.

At one point, usually about five minutes before the hour is up, the secretary of the meeting will call the sharing to an end, make a few announcements about housekeeping or CMA business, and then have someone lead the meeting out with the Serenity Prayer.

"God, grant me the serenity to accept the things I cannot change, the courage to change the things I can, and the wisdom to know the difference. Amen."

And the meeting is over. All in just under an hour.

But don't forget the "meeting after the meeting," where a group of people stand around and talk with one another. Often, some of the group go out for pizza or coffee. This is called "fellowship." It's a great way to get to better know the people in your CMA group.

Slogans, Slogans... and more Slogans

At just about any 12 Step meeting you'll hear them. Take it one day at a time... easy does it... stick with the winners... this too shall pass... meeting makers make it... what other people think of me is none of my business... and so on.

Oftentimes these slogans seem overly simplistic, like something designed for a bumper sticker instead of a serious recovery program. But here's the thing.

Like it or not, they generally offer some pretty good advice. I know it took me several months to stop resenting the robotic way people repeated these clichés at meetings. But eventually I began to hear the message beyond the slogan and I learned a lot.

So expect the slogans, but try to hear the deeper wisdom beneath the shallow surface of the bumper sticker. There's powerful truth in there.

Can I "Pass" If I'm Called On to Share?

Absolutely. Don't worry about having to share if you don't want to. If it's a "round robin" meeting or if you are called upon by the leader to share—which can sometimes happen if no one is volunteering—you can always respond, "I'm new and I think I'll pass for now." No one will judge you.

What About "Clean Time"?

A few meetings, definitely in the minority, ask that you state your clean time when you self-identify. This is to show the newcomer that it's possible to attain longtime sobriety. You'll hear people with a couple of years under their belts, some with 6 or more. If you have less than 30 days, you'll usually get applause for being present. Again, at CMA they remember how difficult are the first 30 days. (Getting your 30 day chip is a *really* big deal in CMA.) If you don't want to say how many clean days you have, you can always say, "I'm [name], a crystal meth addict, and I have today." This is fine, too. I know recovering addicts with years of sobriety who, when asked to state their clean time, always say, on principle, "I have today."

Again, usually, most meetings do not ask for you to state your clean time so it's not an issue.

What Are The "12 Steps" Anyway?

The 12 Steps are the core of any program based on the principles of the Alcoholics Anonymous. A lot has been written about the 12 Steps—literally, shelves of books—but all you need to understand here is that, at one point in any 12 Step recovery program, you will "work" through the steps with a sponsor (a fellow addict whose done them himself/herself).

They are posted on a sign in just about every meeting hall.

The steps have worked for hundreds of thousands, if not millions, of addicts since the 1930s. They can work for you, too. The main goal in completing the 12 Steps is to bring about a "personality" change that's powerful enough to transform your life of addiction into a life totally free from crystal meth. Honesty, open-mindedness, willingness are all that's required.

Know you don't have to start working the steps right away. Attend a few meetings. Get the feel for things. You'll know when it's time to find a sponsor to help you "work the steps." Until then, just keep an open mind and listen to what people share in the rooms about how the Steps are helping them stay clean.

How To Find "My" Meeting

You usually have one meeting that you consider your "home group," which is the meeting that's primary to your recovery, that you don't miss no matter what. Sometimes your home group is the first meeting you attend. Sometimes you'll try out many different meetings before you find just the right one.

Remember, "meeting makers make it." It's not unusual for a newcomer to attend at least one meeting a day.

The rule of thumb is to give a new meeting at least half a dozen tries before you decide one way or the other. Recovery experts believe it takes six meetings before you can accurately understand a group's particular dynamics and tone.

What if I Don't Like 12 Step Meetings?

There are other types of group meetings for people seeking recovery. The most common are those lead by a counselor/facilitator. Many of these, however, are part of an out-patient recovery program that you'll also be required to attend.

The best advice I can offer if you just don't like 12 step meetings is: keep coming back anyway. This is how you can make new sober friends. You don't have to get a sponsor and start working "the steps" in order to attend the meetings. As it says in the selected readings, the only requirement for membership in CMA is the desire to quit crystal meth. Period.

In summary...

Go, force yourself out of your comfort zone. Introduce yourself. Really, where else are you going to meet so many recovering tweakers?

Chapter 5

The Wall

6 Weeks – 4 Months

You hit it hard. All the positive, forward momentum from the Honeymoon crashes around you.

A seemingly insurmountable Wall of depression, boredom, and despair—it usually begins about 45 days into sobriety and it continues through month 4 or thereabouts. Rarely, however, does the Wall last longer than month 6. So, keep in mind, it's going to get better.

The Wall is often where people will relapse. You so want the feelings of boredom and loneliness to pass, crystal meth seems like the solution again. Though the danger of picking up is highest here, you can get past it.

Let's look at what to expect and what you can do to get through this stage of your recovery. The Wall is not impossible to overcome, just tricky.

It feels like hell. If life's going to be like this,
why not use?

— Tim, 3 months clean

Don't isolate. Call people.

— Billy, 1½ years clean

WHAT TO EXPECT

Exhaustion, Loneliness, and Boredom Return

You feel unfocused in life, bored by it all. Not only are you emotionally low, but you're physically spent. Instead of the energized life of the Honeymoon, you're overcome with exhaustion and sluggishness. You may feel intense bouts of loneliness.

This Wall is normal. Expect it. Know it's coming.

Usually, you begin to feel much better between months 4 to 6. So hang in there. You will indeed feel energetic and hopeful again. Don't let the boredom, loneliness, and sluggishness be an excuse to use. In fact, the Wall is the result of your brain and body healing. It's actually a sign that your brain is getting better. You need only keep moving forward, and not give in to your disease's temptation of escape.

What If I Don't Ever Feel Pleasure?

What if you feel no joy in life whatsoever? This profound inability to feel pleasure is a common consequence of prolonged meth use and usually begins about 1½ months after quitting. This can last through months 4 to 6. It's so common, in fact, there is a name for it—anhedonia.

It's tempting to say, "If this is how it's going to feel to be sober, I might as well use again. I certainly can't live this way forever." What you need to know is this temporary lack of pleasure is normal. Again, not only will it pass in a few months, it is actually a sign that *your brain is healing* and to be expected. Ride it out. Like the boredom and loneliness, your pleasure flatline won't last forever.

Using Fantasies, Flashbacks, and Euphoric Recall

In your using years, your body and brain get accustomed to high levels of stimulation. And once you hit the Wall, your brain is not a happy camper. It wants the fast-paced party back immediately. In short, your motto becomes: "I want more, now!" So what happens?

Your cravings for crystal return in full force. Thoughts of using or risky sexual fantasies can become obsessions. You want the rush of excitement crystal used to bring you. Anything to get past the boredom, loneliness, and depression.

The problem with these using fantasies and flashbacks is they are usually incomplete. It's called "euphoric recall." You recall only those exciting, fun and stimulating parts of using—and conveniently forget the overwhelmingly awful side of the experience. You recall half memories, at best.

Euphoric recall is the grand lie of your disease. It wants you only to remember the energy and excitement. Expect this lie—and don't be fooled. You know better. Recall the entire memory, down to the gritty, ugly end of your using days.

Sexual Appetite Spikes

"I want more, now!" translates into a spike in sexual appetite. If you've had relatively low sexual urges thus far, that will most likely change at some point during the Wall. Perhaps it's because the pleasure pathways of the brain aren't functioning and so you desperately want to jump start pleasure. Regardless of the emotional or biochemical reason behind this spike, your sexual appetite usually comes back with a vengeance.

Be careful. Many a recovering addict started using again because of sex. For gay men, it's the number one reason for relapse. I suspect the urge is just as strong for heterosexual couples, as well. (Of course, it is.)

Later in this chapter, we'll take a closer look at sex. (See "Goodbye Crystal Sex, Hello Sober Sex" at the end of this chapter.) For now, just know that, if it hasn't already, your sexual appetite is soon to spike.

Nerve Misfires or Jolts

On occasion, you may get a "jolt" through your body. It's the same kind of jolt you get just before you drift off into sleep and half-dream that you're falling over—and you jolt awake. In a wholly non-medical capacity, I call this a "nerve misfire."

I've seen recovering meth addicts start to sit in a chair and literally miss the chair because of a jolt. Don't be embarrassed. They are usually few and far between and will lessen, and eventually end, within a few months.

Getting an Earful from Friends and Family

Just when you are starting to recover somewhat and no longer feel like Frankenstein's monster, others notice your improvement and suddenly decide it's time to have that blunt conversation about your using. In short, you're just well enough to get dumped on by otherwise well-meaning friends and family.

Try not to bite their heads off.

If you can muster the patience, explain that you are not well enough to have this conversation. You know they care. But now is not the time for any deep, serious conversation about anything, especially your using.

Excuses and Justifications to Use Increase Ten-Fold

I can't emphasize it enough: it's in this period of your recovery where relapse is most common—and there is a reason. Your body is no longer producing the higher levels of dopamine that it did during the Pink Cloud. You've come up against a biochemical wall in your brain—and only time, because that's how the brain heals, can resolve this issue. But since your brain is screaming, "I want more, now," your disease jumps in with some grand excuses and justifications for why now is a good time to "use just a little bit" or "only once more" to alleviate the boredom and loneliness. Here are some of the disease's favorite relapse lies:

It's only for this one time.
I've quit for three months, isn't it time I gave myself a little reward.
If life is going to suck like this forever, I might as well use again.
I can hangout with an old using buddy. If he uses in front of me, I'll just refuse.
My hookup can use crystal because I'll be able to refuse.
I'll go ahead since it's only for this one time.
A little line for energy isn't the same as smoking or slamming.
No one will know, so why not use again? Just this once?

It's important to remember, you have one of the few diseases in the world that tries to convince you that you don't have it.

WHAT TO DO

Prioritize Meetings

According to recovery professionals, the main reasons that crystal meth addicts relapse are boredom and loneliness.

That means to keep from relapsing you need to: 1) keep busy and 2) keep the company of sober friends. Which translates, basically, into... you need to attend a lot of meetings. In AA they have a saying, "Meeting makers make it."

As you start getting better, it's easy to think, "I'm doing so well, I can cut back on my CMA (or AA) meetings and focus on other things." Beware of this kind of faulty thinking. Usually, when a little voice tells you to stop going to meetings that are helping you keep sober, it's your disease talking. The truth is: you need to keep busy, which means making room for all those meetings *first*.

The bottom line is you must put your recovery first, which for now means putting meetings first. It's the fellowship of your sober friends (who *really* understand you) that keeps you from being lonely. And it's attending a meeting a day, or more, that keeps you busy. This may seem like a lot, but it's only your life we're talking about here. And your life is worth the effort.

Let's say it again: meeting makers make it.

Keep Avoiding High-Risk People, Places, and Things

If you've not yet deleted all your old using contacts, or have kept some of those online accounts on hold instead of deleting them altogether, now is the time.

What are the high-risk people, places, or things in your life? Old using friends? Online communities? Dance clubs, sex clubs, or bars? Certain streets or parts of town? Certain movies or television shows that romanticize using?

There's another saying in AA that goes: *If you hang around a barbershop long enough, you're gonna get a haircut.*

Just because you've got a few months of sobriety under your belt doesn't mean you no longer have to avoid high-risk people, places, and things.

Exercise and the Gym

In this stage of your recovery it is vital to begin exercising regularly. Exercise is not only for your body's muscles. Meth's effects can be particularly long lasting and harmful to the brain. Studies by Harvard psychiatrist John Ratey, M.D., show that a fast-paced workout increases the production of specialized brain cells that affect learning and memory. He found that regular exercise not only relieves anxiety and mild to moderate depression, it literally *helps the brain heal faster*. And, just as importantly, a fast-paced workout actually helps redirect the brain away from cravings and fights off the impulse to use – often for hours. Important information to remember.

So, as a recovering meth addict you exercise for three reasons: 1) it's good for your body and overall well being; 2) it assists your brain in healing faster; and 3) it helps counteract the impulse to use.

Should you exercise? Duh.

One other scientific fact it helps to know: it takes 21 days for your brain to create a new habit. If you are at day 18 of exercising and you think, "This is useless and I hate it," stick with it through day 21 and, most likely, you'll feel differently.

Join a gym or an exercise class and give it at least 21 days. This is the new you in recovery.

Keep Busy – Declare War on Boredom

Boredom is the great enemy of sobriety. Start to keep a busy calendar. Set up coffee dates with as many of your non-using friends as possible. Go out to eat

or to the movies. (If you're like most tweakers, you haven't been to a restaurant or movie in ages.) Keep yourself busy. Here are just a few good ideas:

Volunteer for a non-profit organization. This is the best because it not only fills the empty time in your day, but gives you a sense of doing something worthwhile and builds self-esteem.

Join an art class, or some kind of group activity that meets regularly.

Up the number of CMA or AA meetings you go to in a day. Take "commitments" at those meetings.

Go to the gym or take a yoga class.

Start a creative project—painting, writing, dancing, singing or whatever floats your boat creatively.

You get the picture. Keep yourself busy. Make plans and fill your calendar with commitments of one kind or another—and then keep those commitments. As the old saying goes, "An idle mind is the Devil's workshop." In this case, it's very true. So declare war on boredom and inactivity.

Schedule Medical and Dental Checkups

In the first year of your recovery, see your doctor every three months to update him or her on your progress. Be sure he or she knows you were a meth addict and the truthful extent of how much and how long you used. Only in this way will your physician be able to make sure you get the proper care you need. Make your doctor an important part of your sobriety team.

If you were negative for HIV and Hep C, get tested again several months into your sobriety.

If you haven't yet scheduled that dental exam, do so now.

Collect Milestone Chips at Meetings

At CMA or NA meetings they give chips for various lengths of sobriety. There's a "welcome chip," often called the "24 hour chip," then a 30, 60 and 90 day chip. Then comes the 6 month chip, the 9 month chip, and another big one—your first birthday in sobriety—the 1 year chip.

The reason it's important to take these chips publicly is two-fold. First, it's important to honor your sobriety for yourself and your friends. And, second—and maybe this is even more important—it's important to show the newcomer who's only got a few days that, yes, it's possible to quit crystal meth.

Remember when you were the newcomer with only a few weeks of sobriety under your belt? Remember how amazed you were to watch others take their 30 day or 6 month chip?

Those chip-takers at meetings weren't just taking their milestone chips for themselves. They were taking it for the newcomer, you. Now that you're no longer a newcomer, you can return the favor.

Safety in Numbers

It's true and you know it is. Hang around sober people. Hang around recovering addicts like yourself. Also don't live your sober life in the closet. Of course, not everyone in your life needs to know you were a crystal meth addict, but a significant number of your closest friends should know. You need people who will support you in your sobriety, not enable you in denying your addiction.

If a friend doesn't know you are a recovering addict, they are much more likely to accidentally enable bad behavior. To your closest friends, come out of the recovering addict closet. It'll make you closer.

Goodbye Crystal Sex, Hello Sober Sex

If you combined sex and crystal, sober sex might seem overwhelming at first. But thousands of recovering tweakers have relearned how to have healthy—even hot—sex without crystal. It's just going to take some time and effort.

Though, this could just as easily be placed in the "Adjustment" phase of your recovery (the next chapter), a brief "how to" on sober sex is included here because it's during this stage of your recovery that the sexual desires often come roaring back in the form of fantasies or cravings. Anything to escape the boredom, right?

First, the harsh fact: *no more crystal sex ever*. Why? Because having crystal sex means putting crystal into your body one more time—and that you can't risk. The reality is there's no such thing as a one-night stand when it comes to crystal. It comes for days, then might not leave for years. You can't afford to take this risk.

Life without meth means life without meth-fueled sex. It's okay, even necessary for some, to mourn this loss.

One complaint you hear a lot from former tweakers is: regular sex seems dull and just doesn't feel as good as it did on crystal. There's a physiological reason for this. After all the repeated and intense dopamine dumps in your

brain, the fibers in the pathway associated with sex are damaged. But just as with most other pleasurable feelings, this will change over time. Your brain will heal and you'll definitely start enjoying sex again. Just remember it takes time and effort on your part.

Also, sober sex is a different kind of sex. Instead of the limit-pushing, intense, compulsive, nonstop-pleasure marathons you used to have on crystal, you'll have normal sex. If this sounds boring to you, it's just because you're still operating from the perspective of meth-fueled sex.

Imagine charting your pleasure on a scale of 1 to 10. If you think back to your *first* orgasm, whether having sex with another person or masturbating, it was probably so intense and amazing that it scored off the charts—say, a 15. But, after a few more sexual experiences, each orgasm no longer felt so new and intense. Orgasm leveled off to where it belonged, near the top of the "normal" pleasure scale, close to 10.

Like that first orgasm, the first time you had sex on crystal was off the charts. But it was much higher than a 15 because it created an unnatural physiological state that the human brain could never reach on its own. In short, that first experience of crystal sex was closer to a 60. By comparison, sober sex quickly became unsatisfying. After repeated experiences with 60-level crystal sex, regular sex felt empty and boring and on the 1 to 10 scale, sober sex probably rated a 3 or less.

It's important to remember this 3 manifests from the distorted perspective of crystal meth—an expectation of 60-level pleasure that the human brain *was never meant to experience.* After quitting meth, regular sober sex may continue to feel like a 3 or less for awhile. However, in time, your perspective returns to normal and sober sex begins to feel enjoyable again. Of course, sober sex will never be as intense as that 60 of crystal sex, but it will again become one of your great pleasures in life.

Your brain adjusts. Trust the thousands of meth addicts who successfully quit before you—the 10 of natural sex will not only be "enough" but amazing in its own right, just as it was intended to be.

So how do you handle sex in sobriety? There is only one rule: no crystal sex. Here are some ideas…

Wait a year. I've heard it said in CMA that, if you are not already in a relationship, it's healthy to stay away from sex for a full year. This gives you time to work on your recovery without the complications of a major trigger.

Don't wait, but keep it sober. On the other hand, in the early days of CMA, it was sometimes suggested that newcomers have sex with members who had some sobriety under their belt—a big "no-no" in AA circles. The rationale was

that, if you have sober sex with a newcomer, at least they're learning to have sober sex and are less likely to relapse with crystal sex. (These were mostly gay male meetings in Los Angeles.)

Regardless, you will mourn the loss of crystal sex. In *Overcoming Crystal Meth Addiction,* Steven J. Lee, M.D., a psychiatrist who specializes in addiction, uses the analogy of a "trip to Antarctica with breathtaking sunrises over colossal glistening snow peaks, unlike anything you could see on this planet" as a way to put the loss of crystal sex into perspective. On the expedition to Antarctica, you face tremendous challenges. Your body and soul take a beating—it's 20 degrees below zero with fifty-mile-per-hour winds and you get dangerously lost for awhile along the way.

But after this long, difficult and very costly journey, you get to experience something few people ever do: the unseen world of Antarctica. Then, like Dorothy in Kansas, the journey is over and you find yourself back home in the normal, everyday world. But you have an amazing memory to carry with you for the rest of your life. Lee writes, "the immense physical effort and financial cost to get there remind you that this is a place not meant for humans to see. That makes the memory that much more precious—the realization that you saw the unseeable."

Once more: unlike most people in the world, you actually experienced Antarctica and still have amazing memories of the journey. But you'll never go back. *Those once-in-a-lifetime peak experiences are over.* "This is an important admission you need to make to yourself," Lee continues, "because any hidden fantasy that one day you will have crystal sex again is a seed that can grow into an uncontrollable craving and a relapse."

You'll have to grieve the loss and accept it—or else risk relapse.

Remember the stages of grieving: denial, anger, bargaining, depression, and, finally, acceptance. These are applicable to your grief over losing crystal sex forever. *Denial:* I don't have to think of "not-having crystal sex" as a forever thing. *Anger:* I want to have that experience again, damn it. *Bargaining:* I can have crystal sex for one night a month, right? *Depression:* No, I can't because crystal doesn't do one-night stands. *Acceptance:* Since I don't want crystal to ruin my life, I'll have to give up crystal sex forever, which is a worthy exchange.

Sex is tricky. And that's the understatement of the year. There's only one thing that's certain: a healthy and active sex life is important to happiness.

So given that, here are three final points to consider about sober sex:

You were emotionally connected to the meth-fueled sex, not to the other person. It's a lie that you were "more connected" to your sex partner while

using meth. Though you might have been *physically* connected while having a wild party, it was actually the meth and sex that you were *emotionally* connected to, not the person. Be honest, your sex partner could have been almost anyone. The meth was the crucial element. In sober sex, you have the opportunity to experience a genuine emotional connection with another person—something you didn't get with crystal.

After you get comfortable with sober sex, you will be able to have those 10-level experiences again and, most importantly, that will be enough. It's true. And don't fall into the trap of thinking normal sex is just a weaker, tamer version of that wild beast crystal sex. Because the truth is that sober sex is a *different animal* altogether. Sober sex has its own rewards of intense pleasure that sex on meth will never have. Remember kissing? Remember going slowly, and feeling that warm glow from happiness you felt as you explored your partner? Remember feeling really connected, looking your partner in the eyes and staring deep into their being? Even though you'll always have your memories of crystal sex, the intense desire to have it again will pass with time. You may have flashbacks and intense memories from time to time, but they will lessen.

What you get to have in sobriety are sober experiences—and that includes sex. Relearning how to have sober sex could be a book in itself. The main tenets are: *don't use no matter what and give yourself permission to change.* Other than using, if you want, you can try everything you did while thwacked out on crystal. But, today, you get to try it sober. Then, if you find that certain sexual practices don't work for you anymore, you can, in a sober and respectful way, change those practices.

Sobriety is not about making our past behavior wrong. Other than using, it's fair game to experiment with your experience—give it a try sober. You may like it. Or you may feel that certain attitudes toward sex no longer work for the sober you. It's not uncommon for the "no strings attached" sexploits of a person's using days suddenly to seem empty and hollow because, in sobriety, you now want something more meaningful—a "connection" to another person beyond NSA. If this happens to you, then, in a sober and respectful way, begin looking for more lasting connections.

Sex does again become a peak experience. It's just that now it's a 10 at best. Now, it's what is humanly possible. Sex could be fabulous enough before crystal. It will be again afterwards, too.

Chapter 6

Adjustment

4 – 6 Months

You've gotten over the Wall safely and it is now mostly behind you. The next stage is called "Adjustment" because that's what characterizes this time period—adjusting, physically, socially, and emotionally, to life without crystal. You get relief from the overwhelming cravings and begin to find life interesting again.

It doesn't have to get any worse. Your life will get better. One day, you'll find yourself laughing and happy again. Promise.

— Joseph, 1 year clean

Surround yourself with lots of clean time, with people who've been clean for awhile.

— Nicki, 22 years clean

WHAT TO EXPECT

Getting Better Through the Rough Patches

As you progress into the first year, your brain will become sharper and more focused. Life becomes manageable again and everything may seem very new. You definitely feel yourself getting better. The heightened emotions, mood swings, and memory loss that persisted for the first few months of recovery are fading, but it's to be expected that you'll still encounter some rough patches.

Try to ride out those rough patches, because no matter how you look at it, your life is definitely trending toward the positive now that you're clean and sober. Keep an eye on the bigger picture, keep an eye on your life's improvement since you quit.

Your life is getting better. Just slowly. And with some rough patches.

Triggers & Cravings Lessen

With time, triggers and cravings generally lessen. Most recovering addicts have fewer cravings as the months add up. Excluding rough patches where everything is more extreme, triggers may happen only every few weeks or so. What used to be a daily occurrence often becomes a weekly occurrence.

First-Time Sober Experiences

Now that you're not using, you get to have—or have again—various "first-time" sober experiences. From sex to holidays to your child's birthday, there are a lot

of very important experiences that you now get to have sober, either for the first time or "again" for the first time. I personally believe each renewed first is to be celebrated as a big deal—because it is. Most likely, you thought you'd never again enjoy some of life's simple pleasures free of crystal. But today, a new world free of meth's bondage literally opens before you.

The process works like this:

You do some action or experience—let's say, for example, sex—and do it sober. After you have the experience, you get to decide if you liked it or not. You make an adult choice and choose if you want to have that experience again in the same way or, perhaps, change it up a bit. Sex is interesting to discuss because, quite often, what worked for us sexually while high, doesn't work so well sober. We're just not in that "dark" place and, certainly, sex doesn't last for five hours anymore. But let's suppose you have your first sober sexual experience and, on reflection, it doesn't "feel right" to you. There's no blame, here. You didn't do something you shouldn't have—as long as you were sober and didn't harm anyone else, it's okay. Sobriety is about finding out who you are again without meth or other drugs in your system. And only one thing is certain: you are a different person now that you're sober.

Without a doubt, many experiences are now going to feel different.

Some of these first-time experiences you'll not recognize until after you've done them. One recovering addict told me she'd forgotten, until she did it again sober, how much she loved to shop every Saturday at the local farmer's market. Again, I like to think of all these experiences as first-time events even if they are not. Because they are all "firsts" as far as your new sober life is concerned.

Pay attention to your new milestone moments. Mother's Day, Father's Day, Christmas, Hanukkah, New Year's Eve, a birth in your family, the first funeral you are able to show up for sober. These are the obvious big moments. But don't forget the little events. The trip to the farmer's market, or your first crisp autumn morning or balmy summer night. These new first-time experiences are a big deal. So celebrate them. That's a big deal.

If you are like me, you never thought you'd get to live life sober again. Life without this awful drug in your body—what an amazing thing to experience all over again for the first time.

Weight Gain

At the beginning of our recovery, weight gain is all good. In the harsh light of sobriety, that "heroin chic" look you'd fashioned wasn't so pretty, despite what your disease kept telling you. Try to embrace your weight gain.

But what about *excessive* weight gain later on in your recovery? One addict said to me, "Now that I've quit meth for a year, I'm 40 pounds heavier than before I started using." The best solution to unwanted weight gain (and what a problem to have compared to meth addiction) is to increase the rate of your metabolism. At this point, consulting a nutritionist would be a good idea.

But for those who don't go the nutritionist route, for whatever reason, here are some simple ways to increase your rate of metabolism. Try eating 5 smaller meals a day, instead of the usual 3 or 2 large ones. Increase your water intake—a lot. It's probably safe to say you could just double the amount of water you drink now. Also caffeinated drinks actually dehydrate you and so don't count. And neither do sodas, we're talking water, period. Eat healthy fresh foods, not frozen. And, finally, this is crucial: exercise daily. Yes, the best advice to rid yourself of unwanted excessive weight is good old-fashioned moderation of calorie intake and regular exercise.

Sleep Normalizes, Kinda

Usually, sometime in the first year, sleep normalizes. For some it's as early as month 2, but for others it can take much of the year. Of course, if you're pre-disposed genetically to sleep problems, you'll have a harder time. I still take Benadryl every night, but insomnia runs in my family.

Eventually, sleep normalizes. *Kinda.*

Sexual Urges Normalize, Kinda

Or, to put it another way, the extreme sexual urges you had during the Wall begin to lessen. Sex is just such a big, messy deal for many of us—it was for me—that it's a relief when this aspect of your sobriety begins to normalize. If it's taking you longer than 6-12 months, let me say: I understand and it's okay.

It took me well into this stage of my recovery before I could begin reintegrating sex into my sober life. But it does happen.

Your sexual urges do begin to normalize. *Kinda.*

Past Feelings Are Going to "Complete" Themselves

As you journey through the first year, you also begin to realize much of what you've lost because of your crystal addiction—the lost friendships and opportunities, the years of life gone forever. This realization sometimes comes with sadness, as we grieve what could have been, especially had meth not ruled our lives for so long a time. This is all a way of saying, there's a lot of grief for loss that occurs during your first year. Probably, you are going to have or experience some intense feelings.

This should be expected and know you are not backsliding in your recovery. You are actually beginning to experience emotions that your meth use repressed. Ultimately, it's a good thing.

Feelings have a beginning, a middle, and an end. During your drug years, you didn't fully experience those feelings. You bypassed them with an emotional high from using. So whatever powerful emotions that were stirred in you—from the death of a parent, the break up of a relationship, the loss of a job or friendship, any powerful emotion from anger to fear to grief—were not completely felt. So it's now, during your first year, that all those incomplete feelings will need to "complete" themselves.

Consequences from the Damages Done While Using

It's also during this Adjustment that you begin to realize the extent of the damages done by your crystal addiction—the destroyed relationships, the squandered and missed opportunities, the pain you caused others. This realization often comes with great remorse. But the flip side is you can actually see clearly now. And now that you can see the consequences from the damages done while using, you can begin to make these right and, definitely, not repeat them.

Again you are faced with completing emotions you would not fully felt and grieving over what you've lost, but there is also a sense of growing hope. Overall, you have to admit: *it's getting better.*

You are looking at your life's larger picture for the first time in a good long while—and beginning to take responsibility. You are beginning to show up for others in life who count on you.

WHAT TO DO

When You Don't Want to Avoid a Trigger: Feel It and Move Through It

The advice to avoid obvious triggers is especially good in the early weeks and months, but the ultimate goal is to be able to handle—to feel and move through—any trigger which comes your way. You can't simply avoid triggers forever. So let's look at an example of a trigger you know is coming—and how you might cope with it.

Suppose large family gatherings usually trigger you. In the past, you've always responded to the pressure of such situations by using. But now that you are clean and sober, there will be family gatherings where you'll need to show up without getting loaded. Let's take an obvious example, a funeral. You'll want to be responsible and support your family. So, how do you handle this triggering situation?

You handle it exactly the same as you would any sudden trigger. You lean on a sober friend.

Instead of calling someone or going to a CMA meeting, you ask your sober friend beforehand to accompany you to the family gathering. If you get a craving, you'll have your sober friend there by your side. You can literally lean on them, if needed.

Knowing you are likely to be triggered, you don't run away. Instead, you prepare ahead of time. You are able to feel the trigger and have your support system in place so you can move through it. There's an old saying that goes: *feel the fear and do it anyway*. It's like that with a trigger you know you must eventually face, better awkward than backward.

As you grow in your sobriety you will become stronger and more able to handle the triggers that life throws at you. You'll prepare by having tools at your disposal—CMA meetings in which to share, sober friends on whom to lean—that help you become the person of character you want to become.

Go Back to Work or School

I'll say it again: according to recovery professionals, the main reasons crystal meth addicts relapse are boredom and loneliness. So go back to work or school as soon as you can without stressing yourself out too much. It's a balance.

Work With a Therapist

If you haven't already begun to, now is definitely the time to begin working with a therapist, as opposed to a drug counselor alone. You have moved from early abstinence, where the problems encountered were mostly physical and about learning to live without crystal, into a more solid recovery—where the problems you face are mostly emotional and personal.

Meth gave you an instant way to escape emotional distress. One hit and nothing else mattered. All worries vanished, problems dissolved. Using meth "changed the channel" from distress to immense pleasure—instantly. The problem you face today in sobriety is how to deal with the painful feelings you formerly escaped by using. How do you cope with emotional distress now that you no longer use? This is a question all good therapists address with their patients.

The truth many therapists working with addicts have come to realize is: the traditional "talk therapy" model that explores the emotional conflicts of childhood has its limitations. Though this form of therapy might be comforting, it rarely brings about an *actual change* in adult behavior. Insight into past experiences can validate the pain you yearn to escape, but it doesn't offer any practical way to change the old, bad behaviors that currently lead to unhappiness and using. In order to change old behaviors, the addict *needs to learn and practice new life skills* that reinforce a whole new set of behaviors.

Psychotherapy focusing on learning these new behaviors is becoming more common in treatment programs today. These therapies include dialectical behavior therapy, acceptance and commitment therapy, and cognitive behavior

therapy. I recommend you find a therapist who specializes in one of these—though, finally, a good therapist is one who imparts skills that actually make a difference in their patients' lives, no matter what form of therapy is practiced.

If you can't afford to see a therapist or don't have insurance that covers therapy, check out local nonprofit organizations to discover what kinds of free mental health services might be available in your area. In Los Angeles, there are several weekly group therapy meetings specifically for recovering crystal meth addicts that are offered at minimal or no cost. Your options are greater in a large metropolitan area, but you never know what your local university or hospital might have to offer until you check for yourself.

Keep Vigilant about Sex Without Crystal

Sex takes many of us back out. Boredom and loneliness, remember. Sex falls into the loneliness category. I mention sex again because it's such an overwhelmingly huge issue for many of us recovering tweakers. And it's an issue that doesn't go away.

Here are some things for you to consider when keeping vigilant about sex without crystal:

If your sex partner has very little time in sobriety, be extra careful. They are much closer to their using days and still have powerful associations between using and sex. When it comes to recovery from crystal meth, it's often the newcomer to sobriety that is most predatory—just because they are more likely to use the drug for seduction.

Also, what about people from your using past who are now in recovery? A good rule of thumb is: if you ever had crystal sex with a person, you shouldn't try to have sober sex with them because it's just too reminiscent of that particular sex-high. You are likely to get triggered.

For most addicts I know who associated using with sex, there's nothing more difficult than navigating sexual issues. It's an ongoing concern. Work with a counselor or therapist. Seek out new venues in which to find sex partners that are sober—like an AA or CMA meeting, not to mention sober conventions. Some cities have "sober coffeehouses" that cater specifically to those in recovery.

Now might be a good time to reread the earlier section "Goodbye Crystal Sex, Hello Sober Sex" in Chapter 5.

Make Plans and Keep a Socially Active Calendar

At many rehab centers, clients begin their week by making a detailed, hour by hour, plan of what they wish to accomplish for the following week. They list all 12 Step meetings, gym visits, therapy and doctor's appointments, housekeeping times, along with meals, and any social dates—everything—and get it down on paper. This becomes a kind of a contractual agreement between yourself and the universe. You keep to this busy plan no matter what. Your sobriety depends upon it.

There are two aspects to this accomplishment list. First, you have busily scheduled yourself so that there are not many consecutive hours in any given day that are free—no time to get bored. And, second, you have written it all down so you can consult it from time to time—you have a definite plan. I think this is a good practice to do every Sunday evening. Make out your detailed plan for the following week. If you have any large chunks of free time in any of the days, find something to schedule there instead. Call your sober friends and make fellowship dates—to see a movie or go shopping, to have coffee or hike a trail. Anything will work, as long as it involves being socially active with other sober individuals. But fill up that calendar.

It seems simple because it is. Keep a busy schedule and keep socially active. Make plans to do so and follow those plans. Do this and your temptation to use will be minimized.

Chapter 7

Ongoing Recovery

6 – 12 Months

Toward the end of the first year clean, crystal meth addiction can seem distant and almost tangential to your life. Or, it can be something you continue to think about, fleetingly, almost every day. Like all things on this timeline, it depends.

I like to call this part of the quitting journey "Ongoing Recovery" (also known as the "Resolution" stage) because, despite how foreign your crystal dependence may seem, it's important to remember that meth addiction is a "chronic disease" and you are never cured.

Recovery is always ongoing.

It took me fifteen years and eight tries,
and it still wasn't until the pain of using
exceeded the pain of not using that I finally
surrendered.

— Steve, 4 years clean

WHAT TO EXPECT

Triggers and Cravings Out of Nowhere

Yes, this still happens. Just not as often. Perhaps you are no longer triggered by the songs you listened to while using, no longer triggered when driving through the neighborhood where your dealer lived, or by money to spend on payday. Time has worn the edges down and meth's reminders are not so prickly. For whatever reason, you just aren't triggered nearly as often as you were in early sobriety. You haven't had to use the techniques of "thought stopping" and "playing it forward" for weeks at a time, maybe even months.

Still, it will happen. Out of nowhere, you're triggered and find yourself fantasizing about getting high and you're glamorizing the ritual of how you used, remembering only the euphoric bliss of the rush.

You are not backsliding. It might be difficult to remember, but you are still less than a year clean. It takes a solid 2 years for the brain to heal completely from meth use. You're not halfway there. Cut yourself some slack and, when you have cravings, use the tools at your disposal. Stop the thought before it goes further. Or play that tape all the way through to the gritty, disgusting last day of your final run.

And then go to the gym to get some strenuous exercise. You know what to do.

Well Deserved Pride

I hope you feel some pride in what you've accomplished so far in your recovery. Getting clean of crystal meth is no easy feat. It takes persistence, courage, and

strength. At your next CMA meeting, when you self-identify as "I'm a crystal meth addict," feel some well deserved pride in yourself. You've taken your life back. And those of us who are also on the recovery journey know just how difficult it's been.

Even though life may still be a struggle some days, take some pride in what you've accomplished—over half a year clean.

A year is just around the corner. One day at a time, of course.

And Still, My Disease Whispers Its Favorite Relapse Lies

Just because you've got some sober time doesn't mean your disease has gotten any less clever. Your disease is a master at manipulation and will eagerly use your recovery time against you. Here are just a few of its favorite relapse lies:

Partying for one night is not a real relapse.

It's been over six months now. You deserve a night off.

Snorting a line to get this project finished is not the same as partying.

You've proven that you can stop whenever you want. You've got control now.

What's the use of racking up all this clean time, if you're not going to celebrate with a party every once in a while?

You can recover on Sunday and be ready for work on Monday. No problem.

You're going to be out of town, away from your sober friends and family all week. Isn't it the perfect time to take a little party break?

It's not real using as long as you don't slam again. Smoking or snorting isn't nearly as serious.

Of course, you can have a drink. It won't end up with a drunken phone call to your dealer. You're an addict, not an alcoholic.

You get the idea. Remember, just because you've got some time under your belt doesn't mean your disease doesn't still want to kill you. It does.

WHAT TO DO

Put Recovery First

After half a year of sobriety, when life gets busy and full, it's tempting to let your recovery take a backseat. That's a big mistake. Don't forget you have one of the few diseases in the world that tells you, repeatedly, that you don't have it.

One sober living house I'm familiar with here in Palm Springs has each resident answer the following question at their daily check-in each evening: *What did I do today to put my recovery first?* If there's not much on the list, you don't get shamed, but asked to question deeper. Where's the room for improvement? What can you do tomorrow to put your recovery first? I think this is an excellent part of any daily review. Every evening, before you go to sleep, review the day and ask yourself when you put your recovery first. Also, be fearless about looking at when you put your recovery on the backburner. Did you miss a 12 Step meeting for a sporting event on TV? Did you skip your daily meditation because you were running late? Did you blow off the gym? (*Daily* exercise is an important part of your recovery, remember?) Again, the goal is not to shame yourself, but to improve your daily routine and practices so that your recovery is strengthened.

Now, as you move into the second half of your first year, it's more tempting than ever to forget that crucial principle of staying sober: *Always put your recovery first!*

Your disease will be whispering other suggestions nonstop. Don't listen. Put recovery first. Especially now that you're getting better.

Get to Know Yourself Again – the "New" Old You

This is an amazing time, often difficult. but always so beautiful because you are not using, because life is becoming more manageable. These first few months to a year are when you get to know yourself again. The real and authentic you had been hijacked by your addiction. You may have even forgotten what life was *like* before you started using. Maybe the life of an addict is all you've known. Or maybe you remember clearly those days before everything went to hell and meth ruled your life. Either way, you are now beginning to know yourself sober.

You have a choice. You'll either take the opportunity to explore yourself while sober, or will avoid personal growth altogether. I hope you choose exploration because getting to know the new and sober you is the best way to strengthen sobriety and stave off relapse.

There are many different ways to go about this "self actualization" route to better knowing yourself. From doing the 12 Steps to traditional psychotherapy, from Native American vision quests to theater games, there are many different and valid ways to explore your growing self. You'll find your own ways.

Later in the first year comes the beginnings of self reflection and the willingness to grow. And if you're not there yet, relax and don't worry. Your moments of extended serenity will increase over time as you get to know the "new" old you and you'll find a program of self-exploration and growth that works for you.

Volunteer

It's good to keep busy. One good way to fill your time with rewarding acts is to volunteer for a local nonprofit organization. From an urban LGBT center to a rural animal shelter, there are many great organizations that could use your time and energy. In just about every larger city and many smaller ones, as well, there's a rehab or recovery center where you can volunteer.

Also, you'll meet other sober people—not many drug addicts do volunteer work—and do some good in your community.

Throw a Birthday Party for My First Year

It may seem obvious, but I'm going to say it anyway. Throw yourself a big birthday bash when you turn "1" in your sobriety. It is an important milestone.

Receive a cake at your CMA or AA home group meeting.

Take a 1 year chip at every meeting you go to for a week following your birthday. Remember, you are taking these chips not only for yourself, but to show the newcomer and those with less time that long-term sobriety is possible.

Chapter 8

A Year and Beyond

Issues and concerns change as you move into multiple years of sobriety. This is a broad overview of a year and beyond…

You just stop. As you stay clean longer, you realize it's *your* choice as an individual as to whether or not you use.

—Jay, 5 years clean

Fear keeps me clean. I'm not afraid of dying. Most addicts aren't. I'm afraid of relapsing… and not making it back. I'm afraid I'll have a stroke and then my sister, who I don't like, will have to wipe my ass while I lie in bed, unable to move, for the rest of my life. That's the fear that keeps me sober today.

— Brian, 13 years clean

WHAT TO EXPECT

2 Years – the Brain's Magic Number

As you move into the second year, life often becomes manageable again and everything seems fresh and new. Your sleep returns to normal, or to whatever is normal for you. You go months and months without having a using dream.

Sometime near the end of your second year, most recovering addicts report they no longer have the mood swings or bouts of strong emotion they experienced in their early sobriety. The probable reason for this is that it takes about two years for the brain to heal from meth addiction. According to medical studies, two years is the magic number wherein the brain rebuilds itself to compensate for the damage done by meth.

This is not to say years 2 and 3 are going to be a breeze—read on. But when it comes to what to expect *physically*, usually they are much easier.

Floundering – A Few Years Into Sobriety

Once into year 3 or thereabouts, many recovering meth addicts report a period of floundering. Several people interviewed for this book stated unequivocally that years 3 and 4 were the hardest. You have gone through the pain and effort to attain physical sobriety and now are left with—yourself.

After the first year is when the work to attain "emotional sobriety" begins in earnest, when a deeper, exploratory psychotherapy with a traditional therapist (not a drug counselor) is often called for. If you've not yet begun to do so, this is when you explore all those emotions and feelings you were stuffing or hiding with your addiction.

This is also when, if you are in CMA or AA, it's important to be working with other addicts who have less time than you. Ask anyone who's been a "sponsor" and they'll say, when it comes to strengthening your own recovery, there's nothing like working with another addict. When you work with another addict, you take back that much more power from your disease and find yourself floundering less.

And a reminder about individuality. Several of the recovering addicts interviewed for this book encountered their period of floundering much later, in years 5 or 6. As with anything you read in this book, the timeline for you might vary considerably. There's only one you.

The point is to expect the period of floundering. It's normal. This is when it's very helpful to talk to someone who has more time than you.

Get their advice on how to move forward or, at the least, wait it out. This period of floundering will eventually pass. As always, the key is not to let the boredom and irritability serve as an excuse to use again.

Triggers and Cravings Mostly Disappear

Yes, this really happens. It's common for people with more than five years of sobriety to say, honestly, that they no longer have using thoughts or cravings. Triggers almost never arise. This seems to be the norm. About five years and you are a different person. Every seven years the entire human body is completely new—every cell has been replaced—so it makes sense that as you near the seven year mark, the old physical cravings would begin to leave.

Long-Term Consequences from Using

One of the big things you get to face in longtime sobriety is the consequences from the damages done while using. A 12 Step program deals with this aspect of your recovery like no other I know. It's why I suggest every addict do the 12 Steps at least once. It makes you look at the consequences from your time of using—and, most importantly, puts you into a process of making amends for those damages whenever possible.

If you can't make amends to the particular person or institution you damaged, you can at least fully acknowledge the carnage at your hand while in the thick of your disease. This needs to be done to further bolster your resolve to stay in recovery no matter what.

WHAT TO DO

Keep Moving – The Escalator Model

Imagine your addiction as an escalator that is constantly moving downward. You stand in the middle of the addiction escalator and what happens? If you don't move your feet, and start walking upward, the rolling staircase will take you lower into the depths of your illness. The moving steps are always downward. You must walk, sometimes run, up the steps just to remain in place. Otherwise the addiction escalator brings you down once again.

Climbing the escalator is the effort you put into your recovery. Eventually, as time passes and you have more sobriety under your belt, the escalator gets easier to climb and slower. As you climb, you move higher up in life, rather than continually walking just to stay in the same place. The lesson of this model is: you can't stop climbing because the escalator is always moving. If you stop climbing—meaning, you forget that you have a chronic illness that can never be cured and, as a result, no longer put your recovery first—the escalator will bring you back down into the depths of your addiction.

The escalator model is good to keep in mind as you get more time—after years, it's an easier climb and less difficult to maintain your current position—but you still can't afford to stop climbing altogether. You are only moving forward or you're moving backwards into the depths of your addiction. If you've been around recovery for a long time you may have heard it expressed like this: *We either grow or we go.*

You have a chronic illness that cannot be cured, but only treated. And treatment involves walking up the escalator, always. You must keep moving.

Don't Use No Matter What

This is the mantra of longtime sobriety. Of course, the problem is that it's just that—a saying. And when in the clutches of an overpowering craving it's probably not going to be enough. But adopted as your life's motto *and added to the other strategies and skills of recovery* you learn, this simple little saying can take on a powerful significance.

And, remember, don't use no matter what.

Deepen Spiritual Life

Though scientists estimate that genetic factors account for between 40 and 60 percent of a person's vulnerability to addiction, there's a part of our disease that we can't explain physiologically. A lot a research has been done into the psychological and environmental factors of addiction and, certainly, these are significant. What we're left with, at the end of the day, however, is a sneaking suspicion that addiction is a disease of the spirit, as well as the body.

Longtime recovery almost always entails a deepening of the spiritual life. And, here, I mean a broadly conceived notion of "spiritual life." It may not even entail a belief in God, *per se*. And you certainly don't need to be religious to be spiritual.

Explore. If you are working a 12 Step program then you are already involved in a spiritual program. If you are meditating, ditto. I can't tell you where to find it. I know one tweaker with over 15 years sobriety who honestly says his religion is Jedi—and he credits this Higher Power for his sobriety. It definitely works for him and I don't know a person who's sobriety I respect more than this man's. The truth is there are as many ways to explore spirituality as there are individuals.

Bottom line: the evidence seems to suggest that an evolving spiritual life is one of the cofactors in longtime sobriety.

Give Back – Pay It Forward

Another hallmark of longtime sobriety is the notion of giving back to other addicts who are still suffering. The programs of AA, NA, and CMA are par-

ticularly insistent on this as a method to stay clean and sober. After a year or so of sobriety, you are expected to become a "sponsor" and actively help others who have less sobriety than you.

But there are many ways to pay it forward.

More than a few recovering addicts have become specialists in the recovery field, actually going back to school in order to have a new career. In fact, most people you meet who work in recovery are recovering addicts of some sort—or have been touched personally by addiction in some profound way.

You could also do volunteer work for a particularly worthwhile charity. Or, if you are an artist, create a work about addiction and recovery. One of my ways of paying it forward is by writing this book. It's very literally part of my recovery process.

There are many ways to give back to life the gift you've received—a second chance, life in sobriety. The key is to give back. To pay it forward.

Chapter 9

What About Relapse?

We don't blame someone with high blood pressure or asthma for the biological malfunction happening in their bodies. And we certainly don't shame them when they have acute flare-ups of their illness. Why is it different for the meth addict? And what is relapse but an acute flare-up of your addiction/illness?

It's important to begin to understand addiction through the medical model so we can jettison the guilt and shame associated with relapses. This is not to excuse or encourage slips, but to be realistic. The fact is that many recovering meth addicts will slip during the journey of their recovery. I slipped and used several times before I finally quit. It's part of many of our stories. The goal for you, here, is to keep that slippage to a minimum.

In this chapter, we look at what to expect when you slip and how to minimize the duration of the relapse and, hopefully, not slip again.

Get help. Get out of guilt. Don't judge
yourself or beat yourself up. The past is past.

— Nolan, 9 months clean

WHAT TO EXPECT

Lie #1: Relapse is a Moral Failure

The statistics aren't pretty. One well-publicized estimate puts relapse rates at 92%. (Rehab centers have countered with their own statistics of meth users who successfully complete rehab – at a 10 to 30% relapse rate.) The statistic that rings true to my experience is one I've heard from several recovery professionals: a crystal meth addict will slip or relapse on average between 7 and 13 times before, finally, quitting.

But what does all this mean for you? First, the good news is you don't have to be average.

You can be the exception. This most recent relapse can be your last.

The key is to: 1) end your relapse as soon as possible, and 2) learn from it so it won't happen again. We'll look at this in greater detail shortly.

The truth. Recovering from crystal meth is a life-long challenge and very few people who are addicted stop using successfully the first time around. I'll say it again: the average is 7 to 13 relapses before success in quitting takes hold.

For most people, learning how to keep off meth is the same as learning a new skill—like riding a bicycle. Do you know many people who learned to ride a bicycle without falling over a few times? And some of us fell many times before we finally learned the skill.

Relapse does not mean moral failure. It is part of recovery for most addicts. I know I seriously tried to stop several times over a four month period before I finally quit. You could say, "Well, Joseph definitely showed poor judgment during those months because he kept picking up." Maybe. But crystal meth profoundly affects

the brain. My brain was hijacked during those four months by a terrorist that didn't want to surrender. In those first few weeks, when the brain's cravings are at their peak, we make impulsive decisions without thinking them through—because we literally can't think them through. Our brains are impaired.

Also, users who smoked or injected their crystal, have extremely severe cravings during recovery.

So, yes. If you relapse it's completely natural for you to feel discouraged, even angry. But don't turn that anger on yourself—or others. Turn it toward your disease. Remember, your disease lies to you about your recovery. You have one of the few diseases in the world that tells you, you don't have it.

Which brings us to the next lie your disease wants you to believe...

Lie # 2: My Previous Progress in Recovery Was Wasted

Sometimes, someone who slips will claim in exasperation, "I lost all my clean time. I'm back to day zero. I have to start everything over." That's just how your disease wants you to look at it—as a huge mountain to climb that's so big, you just might as well not even try again. A more accurate way to look it as is: "I have been sober 20 of the past 21 days. Compared to any other three week period before I came into recovery, this is progress."

Yes, you must restart your sobriety clock and establish a new sobriety date, but you don't lose the lessons learned from your previous recovery time. I'd be willing to bet that your previous clean time experience (be it once or a dozen times) probably helped you come back to sobriety faster this time around. We just don't lose all that clean time experience. It stays, working on us from the inside. That's why it's important to remember, even though you reset your sobriety date, your previous clean time counts. It's there, accumulating wisdom.

Sometimes you'll hear an old-timer say something like, "I have X years continuous sobriety." If you ask them why they phrase it that way, they'll respond that when it comes to the "total number" of sober years accumulated, they have much more—and they don't wish to discount that other sobriety time. It's there, just not continuous.

Look at the last several months, or year. If you have more clean time in the last three months than you have relapse time, focus on that. You are definitely heading in the right direction. Don't beat yourself up.

As they say, Rome wasn't built in a day. And a solid program of sobriety usually isn't either.

(Now, having said that, there's this: *there is an emotional, spiritual, and physical growth that only comes with long-term continuous sobriety.* It's something you'll have to experience for yourself.)

Bottom line—none of this is to encourage or excuse relapse, but you need to learn not to demonize relapse, either.

If it never happens to you, great. No one is happier for you than I am. But, if you are involved in any groups of recovering meth addicts, from CMA to rehab to group counseling, you will see people relapse. You may not relapse yourself, but people you care about will. So be kind to yourself and your fellow tweakers who are with you on the journey to sobriety.

Now, get back into the rooms of AA or CMA. Raise your hand when they ask if there are any newcomers. You have nothing to be ashamed of—in fact, you're one of the strongest people in the room at that moment. I'll say it again: recovering addicts are some of the strongest people I know and, when sober, become men and women of amazing character. Our suffering makes us that way.

Lie #3: Since I've Slipped and Already Have to Restart My Sobriety Date, I Might as Well Party One More Time

It starts off simple enough. "I've used and so I've blown it. I've fucked up everything I'd built beforehand in my sobriety and have to start completely over (lie #2); and, since I'm such a general fuck-up of a person with no willpower or moral center (lie #1), I might as well just say 'to hell with it' and party on. I can come back to recovery in a few days, after the run."

There are several problems with this strategy.

▶   How do you know this run is going to be only a few more days? It could last weeks or months or years—until you either die of a heart attack or stroke, or crash your car while nodding off on, say, day 6?

▶   You haven't actually lost all that sobriety gained beforehand; it's still there along with the wisdom gained and lessons learned.

▶   In order to avoid your shame of using in the first place, you see the options as either: a) shaming yourself further by admitting your relapse/failure; or b) continuing to ignore the whole incident and party like it's 1999. In reality, these are not your only options. You could, for example, jettison the self-judgment, realize you had an "acute flare-up" of your chronic disease, and seek immediate treatment like, say, someone with a heart condition would. The big question would then be: given this relapse, what are my treatment options?

Bottom line is: this is one of the most insidious lies because its goal is to keep you using and using, without hope of quitting. The truth is you can stop any time and the sooner you stop the more likely you are to turn this relapse into a powerful lesson (a turn) along your road to recovery (as opposed, to a major car wreck). The disease wants you to keep using until you die. It will try every excuse possible to postpone your quitting, including shame for having used in the first place.

Welcoming Embraces and Cold Shoulders

I'd be remiss if I didn't mention the "cold shoulders" you might receive from some other recovering addicts when they find out you relapsed. You'd think, when it comes to understanding and having compassion, no one would be more accepting than another addict, right? It should be that way and, often, is. There are many welcoming embraces when you come back from "field research," as relapsing is sometimes called in the rooms of CMA.

But the truth is when people react negatively to your relapse, they are merely scared for themselves and coming from a place of fear. Maybe they put you on too high a pedestal. Or maybe someone once advised them to, "Hang around the winners only." And they don't have the broader perception to see that, by coming back to recovery from your slip or relapse, you are indeed an extraordinary winner. It's their loss. Forgive them, then focus on your own recovery.

There are at least two important lessons you get from a cold shoulder. The first is: the opportunity to respond to someone else's fear with compassion. Really, the person turning a cold shoulder needs your kindness and loving compassion now more than you need theirs. They are closing their eyes to the parts of life and recovery they'd rather not see. This is not solid recovery behavior, but old addict behavior. You know, ignore life and pretend it's not there. The second lesson of a cold shoulder is: you'll have more compassion

and understanding for others who struggle with relapse in the future. Because you've felt the pain of a cold shoulder, next time it happens to someone you know, you'll reach out a warm embrace and soften your heart to them.

You open your eyes. Open your heart. To yourself and to all others who are struggling with relapses.

7 to 13 times—the average with crystal meth. I hope you are above average. There's no reason you can't be. But if you are not, don't beat yourself up.

And when someone gives you a cold shoulder, remember this: *You are not toxic. What's truly toxic is their thought that makes them respond in fear. Not you, my friend.*

WHAT TO DO

Get Immediately Back into Recovery

The sooner you get back to your recovery the better the odds that you'll make it through this slip to quit successfully. Often, we begin a slip by listening to our disease's favorite lie: "It's only for one night. What can that hurt?" I don't know about you, but I've not met many tweakers who were successful in a one-night stand with crystal meth. (For me, at the end, it was five nights. Every time.)

Another great lie from your disease: "You've already slipped this once, so you might as well do another run. You're going to have to set a new sobriety date anyhow. So what's another few days?"

But is it ever just another few days? Get back to recovery as soon as you can. Don't listen to your disease. Remember, it wants you dead.

Don't Dwell on Shame and Guilt

Infants fall down many times before learning to walk upright, but if they didn't keep trying and falling, they'd crawl forever.

Don't dwell on shame and guilt. Ultimately, excessive guilt is just an ego trip. It's not the end of the world as long as you're back into recovery.

And the most important thing to do is…

Try To Learn From This So It Won't Happen Again

Hello? When did this relapse really begin? Here's a hint: the relapse began long before you picked up the pipe, straw, or syringe.

It may have begun when you started flirting with old triggers—certain people, places, or things. Or maybe you started missing meetings. Then you began listening to the lies your disease whispered. You romanticized using and the cravings quickly overwhelmed you. All of this occurred before you picked up the drug itself.

Carefully examine how this relapse came to be, so you don't unknowingly repeat it.

APPENDIX

Resources

Quitting Crystal Meth – The Blog

My website and blog where the conversation about "living the full and free life beyond meth and addiction" continues. I invite you to visit often and let me hear from you:

quittingcrystalmeth.com

Crystal Meth Anonymous

The first place to go when trying to find a local meeting or connect with other recovering addicts is CMA's website:

crystalmethanonymous.com

Other Organizations/Websites

Narcotics Anonymous info can be found at:

na.org

Then, there's the mothership, Alcoholics Anonymous:

aa.org

And for gay men specifically:
tweaker.org

Further Reading

Clean: Overcoming Addiction and Ending America's Greatest Tradgedy by David Sheff (Eamon Dolan/Houghton Mifflin Harcourt, 2013). Based on the latest research in psychology, neuroscience, and medicine, *Clean* offers clear counsel for parents and others who want to prevent drug problems and for addicts and their loved ones no matter what stage of the illness they're in.

Crystal Clear: Stories of Hope (published by Crystal Meth Anonymous, 2011). CMA's first publication, this is a collection of personal stories and essays on doing the 12 Steps CMA style. 109 easily readable pages.

Overcoming Crystal Meth Addiction by Steven J. Lee, M.D. (Marlowe & Company, 06). This exhaustive book covers a lot of excellent information, including harm reduction and the psychology of addiction. Because of it's length, over 300 pages, I think it's more for the professional in the recovery field or the very motivated addict/reader who wants a broader view of crystal meth beyond the "how to" of quitting.

The Velvet Rage by Alan Downs, Ph.D. (Da Capo Lifelong Books, 2nd ed. 2012). If you are a gay man, this book might be considered a must read. Offering practical and inspired strategies to stop the cycle of avoidance and self-defeating behavior, *The Velvet Rage* passionately explores the stages of a gay man's journey out of shame.

About Joseph Sharp

Joseph is author of *Quitting Crystal Meth: What to Expect & What to Do* (CreateSpace, 2013), *Living Our Dying* (Hyperion '96, translated into Chinese, Japanese, Spanish, German) and *Spiritual Maturity* (Penguin 2002, translated into Spanish). He has worked as a dishwasher, short order cook, legal secretary and chaplain for the Infectious Disease Unit at Parkland Memorial Hospital in Dallas, Texas. Living with HIV since 1982, a survivor of cancer, and recovering crystal meth addict, Joseph hangs his hat in Palm Springs, California.

To contact Joseph visit quittingcrystalmeth.com.

On Facebook at Facebook.com/QuittingCrystalMeth.

Twitter @QuittingMeth.

To buy more books visit amazon.com or your local recovery bookstore.

49523819R00070

Made in the USA
Charleston, SC
27 November 2015